TAXING THE RICH

TAXING THE RICH

How Global Elites Use Justice to Keep Power

MARCO DEUROPA

AD
VERITATEM

Published by Ad Veritatem

ad.veritatem@mail.com

Contents

PART III
POWER

PART IV
THE FUTURE

Introduction

WHY NO ELITE PAYS OUT OF GUILT

In recent years, a phrase that for decades belonged to student movements, street rallies, and the final pages of progressive newspapers has suddenly become a reference point for mainstream politics: *taxing the rich*. We now find it in election platforms, in interviews with enlightened entrepreneurs, and in the tweets of anyone eager to position themselves on the "right" side of history. It is a language that has taken the shape of a new public morality: everyone appears to agree that it is necessary, reasonable, inevitable. As if taxing the rich had become not only possible, but downright obligatory.

And yet behind this apparent moral obviousness, something rings false. For if a genuine collective will for tax justice truly existed, pressure on wealth would not be at a historic low, nor would capital be so concentrated at the top. The paradox of our time is precisely this: never before have elites talked so much about the need to tax themselves; never before have they been so successful at avoiding it. The language of justice and the reality of power move in opposite directions, and the distance between them has become the political signature of our age.

This book begins with a very simple question—one rendered almost illegitimate by our dominant moral discourse: *why do the rich want to be taxed?* Is it truly out of guilt, solidarity, or a mature awareness of the system's fragility? Or does the rhetoric conceal a deeper, more refined, more coherent project of power?

The thesis of this book is that no elite pays out of guilt. Elites pay in order to preserve. To stabilize an economic order that, in return, grants them even greater power. In a globalized world, the gesture of "agreeing to be taxed" is not a renunciation: it is a strategy. It is the way new ruling classes reinvent their moral profile, consolidate their leadership, anticipate social crises, and compel states to recognize their centrality. Paying becomes an investment; self-taxation a form of insurance; tax justice an elegant way to reaffirm one's indispensability.

"Taxing the rich" has become a language that consoles the masses and reassures the elites—a ritual that allows society to believe conflict has been addressed, when in fact it has merely been domesticated. Embedded in this language lies the greatest misunderstanding of our time: the belief that redistribution is a moral gesture, when it has increasingly become a tool of governance.

The pages that follow are neither an indictment of the rich nor a defense of inequality; they are an attempt to understand the deep workings of the new economic morality shaping our era. A morality that does not emerge from below but from above; that spreads not through politics but through image; that is not a renunciation of power but one of its metamorphoses. For today's elites maintain their dominance not by hiding, but by displaying their virtue.

Which leads to a different central question: does taxing the rich truly limit their power, or does it instead affirm their leadership in a more sophisticated form?

This book attempts to answer that question.

A Note on the Term "Elite"

Throughout this book I will use the word *elite* frequently. It is a term that circulates everywhere, yet almost never with a clear meaning. For some, it simply refers to the very wealthy; for others, to the political establishment; for others still, to a distant, closed, omnipotent caste. None of these images correspond to what I mean. To avoid misunderstanding, it is necessary to clarify the term from the outset, because the central thesis of this book concerns the elites—not as a journalistic caricature, but as a structural feature of contemporary power.

When I speak of elites, I am not thinking of the "super-rich" in an economic sense, nor of the small minority that owns extraordinary fortunes. Wealth is a marginal aspect of an elite, not its definition. There are wealthy individuals who have no influence whatsoever, and individuals who are not particularly wealthy yet exert systemic influence. The elite does not coincide with the political class either: running a ministry does not necessarily mean wielding real power, and many of today's most influential decision-making centers lie outside the state rather than within it.

By *elite* I refer instead to the constellation of actors—economic, technological, cultural, technical, financial, and at times political—who occupy positions that allow them to shape the functioning of society in a non-episodic way. They do not necessarily exercise this influence by commanding; more often they do so by coordinating, stabilizing, translating complexity. Elites are not a group but a position: the position of those who have access to the levers that regulate information flows, technical standards, digital infrastructures, financial capital, and the framing of public agendas. They do not need to meet in secret to exert power; their power derives from operating within systems that already distribute influence asymmetrically.

The contemporary elite is not a closed caste; it is constantly renewing itself. Twenty-five-year-old technologists, influential academics, global fund managers, algorithm designers, officials in supranational organizations, journalists capable of steering public debate—any of them can become part of the elite. What unites them is not income or lifestyle, but the ability to convert resources—economic, technical, symbolic—into effective power. And such power is measured not by quantity but by continuity: one belongs to the elite when one can influence the course of events even without appearing on the surface.

What characterizes the elite, then, is not wealth but function. They do not govern in the classical sense; they coordinate. They do not impose commands from above but make certain directions of movement possible, probable, inevitable. Even when they appear to be yielding something—for example, when they claim to support higher taxes on themselves—they are in fact fulfilling their role: preventing crises of legitimacy that could destabilize the system as a whole. This is why a clear definition is indispensable. Without it, we risk interpreting as moral will what is often a systemic necessity, and as an ethical gesture what is almost always a mechanism of stabilization.

In these pages, therefore, the word *elite* should not be understood as a moral judgment or an accusation. It is an analytical tool. It refers to those who, by virtue of their position within networks of economic, technological, cultural, or institutional power, can steer collective decisions, set the boundaries of what is possible, absorb crises, and convert them into a new order.

PART I
THE RHETORIC

The Myth of "Tax Justice"

THE STAGING OF FAIRNESS

In almost every Western country, when the media talk about "tax justice," they are not describing a complex reality: they are telling a fable compatible with the rhythms of a talk show and the three-minute breath of an evening news segment. The plot is simple, repeated to exhaustion: on one side stands a "unjust" tax system that allows the rich, multinationals, and the cunning to pay less than they should; on the other side stands the community of "ordinary" citizens, bearing an ever-heavier burden. The solution seems just as straightforward: make the rich pay, close the loopholes, crack down on tax havens, "restore order." In this narrative, tax justice appears as an act of moral cleansing: it is less about understanding how economic power structures actually work and more about intercepting a widespread sentiment—resentment toward inequality—and transforming it into a message that can be spent politically and televised efficiently.

It is a mise-en-scène requiring very few characters: the citizen who "can't take it anymore," the politician who promises reform, the expert who speaks of brackets and rates as if they were pieces of Lego waiting to be reassembled. Above all, it requires a decisive rhetorical gesture: treating taxation primarily as a matter of moral will. If things go wrong, it is because "there was no will" to tax the rich, because "courage is lacking," because "lobbies prevail." This reduction of complexity to a question of courage and intention has a profoundly sedative effect on public opinion: it turns a network of structural relationships—between states and financial markets, between public debt and capital flows, between legal architectures and the concentration of wealth—into a kind of simplified ethical drama, where identifying the villain and invoking a tougher law seems enough.

It is in this simplified, emotional, moralizing space that contemporary tax-justice rhetoric finds its natural habitat: a place where the relationship between taxation, power, and sovereignty is not truly examined, but where small acts of ritual indignation are performed nightly. In this theatre, economic elites can afford the luxury of joining the performance: a billionaire declaring he wants to pay more taxes is presented as a virtuous exception, a symbol of potential change; in reality, his appearance on screen serves to legitimize the idea that the system can correct itself without any need to touch its foundations.

Media-driven "tax justice" does not arise to explain how taxation redistributes or consolidates power, but to offer the public a comforting story: the problem lies in excessive injustice; the solution will come through a painless correction; no one needs to ask who truly writes the rules of the game, which supranational constraints limit the freedom of states, or how the language of rights and equality is absorbed and reused precisely by those who benefit most from deeper continuity.

In this sense, the myth of tax justice begins here: at the very moment the issue is translated into a morally legible and politically harmless story, delivered into the communication circuit as a consumable product—one in which we can denounce the cheats, applaud the "enlightened" rich, and return home with the fleeting sensation that justice, for a moment, appeared on the screen.

THE ROLE OF PROGRESSIVE ELITES

In the contemporary narrative on tax justice, progressive elites occupy a peculiar place: they are not the target of criticism, like traditional economic elites, nor the object of popular indignation; they are, rather, the voice that reassures—the component of power that offers itself as the moral interpreter of injustice. Their function is not to defend the status quo frontally—no modern elite can do that anymore without losing legitimacy—but to propose a form of self-correction that, while denouncing the system's distortions, simultaneously renders them acceptable. In an age in which inequality is visible, measurable, debatable in real time, progressive elites present themselves as those who "see the problem" and offer a way out that requires no conflict, no rupture, no profound transformation: a moral and administrative escape route compatible with the continuity of the existing order.

Their historical role has appeared whenever an economic system has crossed the threshold of social tolerability. When the distance between those who have and those who have not becomes too vast to ignore, a segment of the elite abandons the rigid defense of privilege and adopts the language of justice. Not because it rebels against its own condition, but because it understands that the legitimacy of privilege can no longer rest on silence; it requires a discourse that acknowledges injustice while neutralizing its political consequences. The progressive elite is not the "good" faction of the wealthy: it is the more intelligent one. It is the faction that senses earlier than others that power without an ethical narrative is vulnerable, contestable, exposed to populist or revolutionary drift. And so it undertakes to provide a language that allows power to preserve itself, presenting itself as self-critical, responsible, even penitent.

What distinguishes progressive elites is not a greater inclination toward justice, but a greater ability to speak the language of their time. In the second half of the twentieth century, when welfare appeared to be the natural mechanism of democratic order, many great fortunes embraced the cause of the social state—provided the social state did not interfere with the deep infrastructures of capitalist production. Today, in a fragmented and identity-driven world, dominated by the perception of a "faceless" economic power, ethical demands revolve around transparency, sustainability, and symbolic rather than material redistribution. Progressive elites interpret this language, anticipate it, reinforce it—and in doing so build around their role a moral framework that did not exist in earlier phases of capitalism. They do not relinquish power: they reformulate its moral premises, making it more difficult to attack.

Their strength—and their limitation—is that they know how to make injustice narratable. They can transform a structural fact—the concentration of capital in the hands of very few—into an administrative problem open to moderate adjustments. In this sense they fit perfectly into the rhetoric of tax justice: they do not contest the structure of the system but suggest that by fine-tuning some mechanisms, introducing a few new principles of fairness, increasing progressivity, an acceptable balance can be restored. The implicit message remains constant: the system can heal itself. All that is required is for those who benefit most from it to accept contributing a little more. The real question—whether this system, as constructed, is capable of producing a just society—is pushed aside.

Progressive elites, then, do not represent an alternative to power but its updatable version. They function as a device of adaptation: turning critique into reformism, resentment into moderation, the possibility of rupture into a demand for moralization. Their voice serves to prevent a crisis of legitimacy from becoming a crisis of authority. And when they speak of taxing the rich, they do not do so to challenge the architecture that makes their own existence possible, but to shield that architecture from more radical delegitimization. Their intervention is surgical: correct what risks generating instability; concede what does not compromise the core of power; demonstrate to the public that wealth is not deaf to its suffering, and that no systemic alternative need be imagined.

The role of progressive elites, therefore, is to mediate between the unsustainability of injustice and the impossibility, for the elite as a whole, of renouncing what constitutes it. It is an essential role for the reproduction of order: without them, power would appear too naked, too brutal, too distant. With them, power adopts a voice capable of speaking of justice without questioning itself. A voice that says: we are ready to pay more, provided nothing essential truly changes. A voice that does not ask society to trust the rich, but to believe that the rich can be part of the solution. This, today, is their most advanced form of hegemony.

WHY IT IS NOT A POPULAR MOVEMENT BUT A VERTICAL ONE

Despite its democratic rhetoric, the push behind the idea of taxing the rich does not come from below. It is not the product of a popular movement, nor the spontaneous expression of discontent taking political shape. It is an eminently vertical movement: promoted, legitimized, and administered by those who already occupy strategic positions of cultural, economic, and institutional power. Civil society appears here as the recipient of the message, not its source. And this asymmetry is crucial, because it shows that the goal is not to "give citizens their voice back," but to reformulate the legitimacy of the elites in a context in which their authority has grown fragile.

The vertical nature of the movement emerges from a simple fact: the platforms from which the call to "tax the rich" originates are not public squares but foundations, think tanks, prestigious universities, major newspapers, and the international venues where global governance is discussed. It is not the social groups penalized by an unjust system who organize to demand tax reform; rather, it is the actors who have every interest in demonstrating that the system remains capable of self-correction. In modern democracies, genuine protest is unpredictable, often unruly, irreducible to a unified message; by contrast, the rhetoric of tax justice is surprisingly uniform. The same concepts, the same slogans, the same statistics appear simultaneously in New York, London, Berlin, Paris. This homogeneity is not evidence of popular consensus but of a discursive strategy that spreads through imitation and convenience, not through lived experience.

What makes the movement's vertical character even clearer is the way its narrative is crafted and disseminated: through editorials, well-funded campaigns, international conferences, and media statements by figures belonging to society's upper tier. The ordinary citizen rarely appears except as a symbol, a rhetorical figure, an abstract beneficiary. Inequality is invoked as a moral datum but never translated into the concrete voice of those who endure it. It is a justice spoken from above, describing and interpreting social distress without allowing that distress to articulate itself autonomously. A truly popular movement would be disorderly, fragmented, conflictual. Here, instead, everything is composed, calibrated, wrapped in an almost technocratic language that transforms injustice into an administrative issue.

But the deeper reason the movement cannot be popular is that its outcomes do not address the needs of the majority; they address the needs of the system. A demand arising from below would aim to redistribute power, not merely income. It would call for a different relationship between labor and capital, question the freedom of money to circulate without constraint, challenge the very architecture of global financial markets. It would not simply ask for higher taxes on the wealthiest, but for a broader rethinking of the concepts of wealth and property. The "tax the rich" movement, however, touches none of these points. It accepts the existing structure of capitalism as a natural fact and confines itself to proposing an adjustment—a small pressure from above, presented as a moral sacrifice—that does not require any transformation of power dynamics.

The verticality of the movement is so evident as to be almost its defining trait. Elites do not endure it; they produce it. And they produce it because they have understood that the public no longer believes in the neutrality of the market, the automatic goodness of growth, or the efficiency of traditional institutions. When the old language stops working, power searches for a new lexicon. And tax justice—precisely because it reduces complexity to a symbolic gesture, "we will pay more"—allows elites to reestablish themselves as moral interlocutors of the common good. A genuine popular movement would impose questions that power cannot control. A vertical movement, instead, drains those questions of their subversive charge and returns them to society in a mitigated form, compatible with the existing order.

In this sense, the rhetoric of taxing the rich belongs fully to the grammar of contemporary governance: it is not born to overturn the pyramid but to prevent it from collapsing. It does not give voice to the people; it pacifies them. It does not open new political possibilities; it closes the most dangerous ones. And for that reason, it can only be vertical—proceeding from above, speaking a language that only those above truly understand. The people appear in the narrative as beneficiaries of justice, never as its authors. And this absence, more than anything else, reveals the movement's deepest nature.

The Cultural Roots of the New Economic Moralism

FROM NINETEENTH-CENTURY PHILANTHROPY TO WOKE CAPITALISM

To understand the new economic moralism that today coats power in an ethical sheen, we must trace the long genealogy through which elites have learned, over the centuries, to transform their economic function into a moral mission. Nothing emerges from nothing: today's rhetoric of "doing good," of social responsibility, sustainability, diversity as an ethical value, and of "paying one's fair share" is not a rupture with the past but the result of a slow evolution that has led capitalism to incorporate, as part of its own language, the cultural forms of its own critique. Nineteenth-century philanthropy was the first laboratory of this transformation: it appeared as an act of generosity, but in reality inaugurated a method for controlling, modulating, and directing the social consequences of concentrated wealth. The Victorian industrialists who built schools, orphanages, libraries, and workers' housing did not intend to subvert the capitalist order; they intended to prevent its destabilization. They provided services the state could not yet guarantee and, in doing so, created a bond of gratitude and dependency that made their position less contestable. It was a paternalistic philanthropy: the rich took care of the poor, on the condition that the poor did not question the structure of their own subordination.

This philanthropy did not arise from guilt but from the intuition that economic power, to be stable, must be perceived as beneficent. Wealth without a moral narrative to justify it appears naked, arbitrary, vulnerable. The great capitalists of the nineteenth century understood this well: benevolence constructed from above not only alleviated certain effects of industrial misery but endowed benefactors with an aura of indispensability. They were no longer merely exploiters; they were guarantors of welfare, patrons to whom the community owed recognition. Philanthropy thus produced a double operation: it mitigated conflict and reinforced power.

In the twentieth century, with the expansion of the welfare state, this philanthropic model was partially eclipsed but did not disappear; it merely changed form. The large private foundations that emerged in the United States—the Rockefeller, Ford, and Carnegie foundations—broadened the range of economic power, occupying the spaces left open by the state and presenting their initiatives as experiments in modernization, education, and public health. These foundations acted as geopolitical and cultural actors, shaping entire fields of knowledge and research, yet always under the banner of private generosity. Philanthropy had now become a parallel method of governance: it did not replace the state, but complemented it—often anticipating it, sometimes redirecting its aims. Again, this was not guilt; it was strategy.

The contemporary era has added a new ingredient to this genealogy: the cultural moralization of capital. What we call—using a convenient but insufficient term—"woke capitalism" is the outcome of a long process that has led elites not only to support social causes but to identify with them as part of their own moral identity. This capitalism does not merely fund hospitals or universities; it claims to embody values. It promotes inclusion, diversity, gender equality, minority rights, the fight against climate change. It is a capitalism that speaks like a social movement, that appropriates the vocabulary of justice, that produces campaigns, narratives, symbolic rituals. For the first time, economic power does not merely present itself as benefactor: it presents itself as moral guide.

This metamorphosis does not arise from an ethical awakening but from a crisis of legitimacy. When financial markets become global, when states lose control over value chains, when inequalities explode in visible and statistically undeniable ways, economic power understands that it can no longer rely on the old justification of growth. "Prosperity for all" is no longer credible. Elites must find another source of legitimacy: they must become the moral interpreters of their time. Woke capitalism responds to this need: it does not simply correct the system's side effects; it reinvents its internal narrative. It makes justice an attribute of corporations, sustainability a brand, inclusion a service. And thus it transforms the critique that once came from below into a symbolic resource usable from above.

The shift from nineteenth-century philanthropy to woke capitalism is therefore not a moral evolution but a technical sophistication. In the former, power donated services; in the latter, it donates values. In the former, it built schools; in the latter, it builds political identities. In the former, it asked for gratitude; in the latter, it seeks moral recognition. The new economy of virtue does not simply distribute resources; it redistributes meanings. It offers the public the image of a power that not only produces wealth but justifies it through its adherence to ethical causes. In this way, the conflict between capital and society is translated into a language that does not require antagonism but moral convergence. The new elite does not oppose ideals of justice; it incorporates them. And by incorporating them, it neutralizes them, making them compatible with its own function.

It is in this context that we must read the contemporary rhetoric of tax justice: as the latest incarnation of a historical process through which elites transform morality into a technology of power. They do not repent; they update. They do not correct the system; they make it more elegant, more symbolic, more difficult to contest. Industrial philanthropy gave bread; woke capitalism gives values. It is an apparent moral progress, but a real refinement of the same logic: transforming justice into a language that power can speak without calling itself into question. The rhetoric of "paying one's fair share" is merely its most recent—and perhaps its most sophisticated—expression.

WHY ELITES MUST APPEAR "GOOD"

In contemporary societies, economic power can no longer afford to be merely powerful. It must also be good—or at least appear to be. This necessity is not a communication strategy, nor an accidental consequence of media culture. It is a structural condition of the age we live in. Elites must appear good because their legitimacy can no longer rest on traditional authority (as it did for aristocracies), nor on the tangible collective benefits produced by the system (as during Fordist capitalism), nor on the unquestioned technical superiority of markets (as in the decades of triumphant neoliberalism). Today, none of these three pillars stands on its own. Growth no longer distributes well-being in a credible way; institutions are perceived as fragile; markets as impersonal powers without responsibility. Faced with this erosion of the symbolic foundations of economic domination, elites need to rebuild an affective relationship with society, to present themselves not as the cause of suffering but as the moral agents capable of alleviating it. They must appear good because it is the only way, today, to appear legitimate.

Power has always required moral narratives, but only in certain eras do those narratives become integral to its daily functioning. Ours is one of those eras. In hyperconnected societies, where every gesture made by an influential actor is instantly visible and subject to judgment, morality becomes a precious resource—an immaterial capital without which decisions lose authority and become suspect. If once it was enough to say, "we create wealth," today this no longer suffices. One must say: "we create wealth, and we do so for the good of all." This shift is unavoidable because the very image of wealth has cracked. It is no longer seen as the natural product of merit or individual initiative, but as the outcome of an opaque system, of global mechanisms beyond democratic control, of asymmetries no one can convincingly justify. When wealth loses its aura of inevitability, it must recover an aura of goodness.

For economic elites, the need to appear good therefore answers a need for protection: protection from suspicion, from anger, from political and judicial interpretations of their position. A society that sees the rich as morally hostile or indifferent to its problems may tolerate them for a time, but no longer considers them necessary. And when an elite ceases to be perceived as necessary, the process of delegitimization begins. Woke capitalism, mediatized philanthropy, the rhetoric of social responsibility, the insistence on tax justice as an ethical gesture—everything arises from this primary need: elites want to avoid being perceived as superfluous or harmful.

That elites appear good serves above all one purpose: to prevent social conflict from taking political form. In Western democracies, adherence to shared moral values is one of the most effective ways of neutralizing the possibility of real antagonism. If economic power can convince society that it is already "doing its part," that it is not shirking its duties, that it understands the difficulties of the vulnerable, then the question of what is truly just will not become a political program but will remain confined to the ethical register—where it can be managed through statements, campaigns, institutional partnerships, small fiscal adjustments. A moral gesture is infinitely cheaper than confronting a material conflict. Virtue, when offered symbolically, costs far less than the real redistribution of power.

But there is a deeper level still, one that has less to do with strategy than with the mental structure of contemporary capitalism. Elites must appear good because they operate in a world in which the language of goodness has become the dominant grammar of institutions. Companies can no longer call themselves merely efficient: they must call themselves just. Investors can no longer call themselves farsighted: they must call themselves sustainable. Digital platforms can no longer call themselves innovative: they must call themselves inclusive. The economy is no longer presented as a neutral system of resource allocation, but as a moral arena in which everyone must declare who they are, what they defend, what they are willing to do for others. This moralization does not arise from religious fervor but from the need to cloak in values a system that would otherwise appear for what it is: an impersonal structure that produces enormous advantages for a few and diffuse costs for many.

Elites must appear good because goodness has become the new form of power—a power that no longer wishes to impose itself by force, nor justify itself through technical expertise, but spread through symbolic consensus. Goodness is a technology: a technique for governing the social imaginary. Through it, wealth does not merely exist; it explains itself, justifies itself, presents itself as a solution. And in this movement, the very possibility of questioning its origin or its concentration becomes increasingly remote. Moral power is the most effective form of power because it does not appear to be power at all.

This is why elites must appear good: not because they are good, not because they desire goodness, not because they seek to be loved, but because without goodness they could no longer govern a society that has ceased believing in the neutrality of wealth. Goodness is not their attribute; it is their mask. And like every effective mask, it does not conceal what one is, but transforms what others are permitted to see.

PART II
REALITY

Why the Rich Want to Be Taxed

SYSTEM STABILITY

When the rich declare that they want to be taxed, the most naïve interpretation is also the most widespread: that it is an act of justice, a moral awakening, a late recognition of their responsibilities. The reality is both simpler and deeper: elites support higher taxes on themselves because they know that the stability of the system from which they benefit is beginning to waver. It is not a gesture of altruism but of preservation. In every historical era—from the European aristocracy of the late eighteenth century to the industrial magnates of the early twentieth—the ruling classes have accepted concessions whenever they perceived that the cost of rigidity would exceed the cost of giving something up. Progressive taxation, in this sense, is the price of order. It is an apparent sacrifice that makes it possible to avoid real sacrifices: revolts, draconian wealth expropriations, irreversible political ruptures.

System stability is not an abstract good that elites defend out of civic duty; it is the very condition of their existence. Their wealth does not survive in a vacuum. It depends on solid institutions, predictable markets, functioning infrastructures, confidence in money, the law, the state. When this fabric begins to fray, even great fortunes become fragile. Elites, who live in constant contact with economic indicators, capital flows, market moods, and government signals, perceive destabilization long before the general population. They sense rising public discontent before it becomes protest; they feel the growing unpopularity of wealth before it crystallizes into political demands; they grasp the weakness of states before institutions admit it publicly. This is why they speak of taxation: not out of generosity, but prudence.

When a system is in equilibrium, the rich do not ask to be taxed; when the system trembles, they suddenly become champions of tax justice. It is only an apparent paradox. The true motive is not redistribution but continuity. Taxing themselves means making an economic model sustainable that would otherwise risk being overturned—exposed to more radical contestation, vulnerable to populist policies or authoritarian turns that could endanger not only wealth but its transmissibility. Better to concede a portion of the surplus than risk the total delegitimization of the surplus itself.

Taxation accepted by elites thus functions as a form of political insurance. It acts as a social shock absorber that prevents the system from overheating. Increasing the fiscal burden on large fortunes by a few percentage points is infinitely less costly for them than facing a context in which the social contract breaks down and wealth is perceived not as an aspiration to emulate but as an injustice to punish. Instability is the great fear of the rich —far more than poverty. Poverty barely concerns them; instability concerns them completely.

The stability elites seek, however, is not only economic: it is symbolic. In a society that perceives itself as unjust, wealth becomes an emotional target; in a society that perceives itself as protected, wealth becomes an acceptable price to pay. Progressive taxation then works as a symbolic therapy: it softens resentment, allows people to believe that the system is "correcting its excesses," and offers a narrative of balance that preserves order without altering its structure. Nothing is more advantageous for an elite than a widespread perception that the system is unjust but improvable, harsh but reformable, unequal but not irredeemable. It is this perception that neutralizes radicalism and turns protest into patience.

This is why the rich want to be taxed: not because they believe in justice, but because they believe in the continuity of the system that sustains them. Taxing themselves is the way they purchase time, consent, stability. It is an implicit pact that says: "we agree to contribute more, as long as the structure of our privilege remains untouched." It is a rational choice, not a moral one—a form of preventive maintenance: inexpensive, and powerfully protective. It is the ethics of power disguised as the ethics of responsibility.

MORAL LEGITIMATION

If system stability represents the structural reason elites accept being taxed, moral legitimation is the symbolic one—and in the contemporary world, perhaps the most decisive. Economic power can no longer present itself as a natural fact, nor as the inevitable consequence of merit, competition, or efficiency. Those narratives, which for decades served as ideological shields, now collapse against an increasingly visible truth: extreme wealth does not arise from a neutral world but from a system of rules that selects, concentrates, and protects capital. Once this awareness spreads, wealth no longer appears as the product of individual ingenuity but as the outcome of structural conditions of advantage. And what is structural cannot be justified through the psychology of merit. To survive, it must be cloaked in morality. Voluntarily accepted—or publicly demanded—taxation becomes a tool of self-absolution: a way to convert privilege into a form of public responsibility.

The essential point is that economic power does not merely want to avoid being hated; it wants to be regarded as necessary. And to be regarded as necessary today, it must appear morally credible. Competence is no longer enough; efficiency is no longer enough; innovation is no longer enough: goodness is required. Moral legitimation has become the symbolic currency without which wealth cannot circulate in the public sphere without being ceaselessly questioned and contested. Hence the insistence on formulas such as "giving back," "contributing," "paying one's fair share": these are not expressions of altruism but the lexicon of a new self-narration through which dominant actors present themselves as active participants in the common good rather than detached beneficiaries of it.

The process is subtle but powerful. By accepting higher taxation, elites do not merely stage a gesture of fairness; they reposition themselves symbolically within the moral fabric of the community. They become not only those who accumulate but those who participate. They become "exemplary taxpayers"—a carefully crafted and perfectly functional oxymoron: exemplary in privilege and exemplary in sacrifice, therefore exemplary in all things. The fiscal act becomes a public declaration of belonging to the community. And if belonging means "participating according to criteria of fairness," then the gesture of taxation serves to evoke—though not to realize—the figure of the moral citizen.

This moral legitimation has enormous political force because it produces a perceptual inversion: wealth, usually suspect, becomes a guarantor of justice; power, normally accused, becomes the defender of the community; the elite, often seen as a body external to society, becomes its ethical pillar. It is a perceptual reversal that neutralizes the very possibility of radical conflict: who could attack those who are already "doing the right thing"? And above all, who could propose a political alternative to wealth when wealth appears as the force sustaining institutions, services, and fiscal stability? If the rich become part of the solution, they can no longer be conceived as part of the problem.

Moral legitimation, therefore, is not an ornament of power. It is its survival environment. Elites have understood that in a world where material distribution can no longer be defended with economic arguments, it must be defended with ethical ones. This is why they insist so much on their fiscal contribution: not to show that they are giving a great deal, but to suggest that without them everything would collapse—that their role is non-negotiable, that their presence is indispensable to the very cohesion of the community. Taxation here becomes the ritual of a new civil religion: money is no longer sufficient to justify power; it must be shown that this money is "good," that it circulates under the sign of responsibility, that it represents not only accumulation but participation.

In this scenario, moral legitimation is the most effective of defenses because it does not present itself as a defense. It presents itself as virtue. And virtue is the most elegant, powerful, and discreet means by which an elite can consolidate its position. It does not merely convince others of its goodness; it convinces them that without that goodness—without that specific, moralized form of power—society would be more unjust, more fragile, more impoverished. The elite does not seek to be loved: it seeks to be regarded as indispensable. Morality is the language through which it strives to persuade the world that it truly is.

PREVENTING THE COLLAPSE OF THE SOCIAL CONTRACT

When elites openly support higher taxation on themselves, what they fear is not the loss of a marginal share of their wealth, but something infinitely more dangerous: the collapse of the social contract that holds society together and that, implicitly, justifies their position. No economic system can endure solely on the strength of its institutions or on GDP growth. Every system, to last, requires a degree of collective acceptance—a minimum consensus that makes power relations appear legitimate, that renders inequality tolerable, and that keeps injustice within the bounds of what is perceived as "normal." When this consensus cracks, power enters a danger zone. And elites, who live at the top of the pyramid, are also the first to see when the base begins to crumble.

The modern social contract rests on an implicit promise: despite inequalities, life will improve, opportunities will be real, the state will provide minimal protections, and sacrifices will be rewarded. This promise held for decades, especially in the postwar period, when economic growth and the expansion of the welfare state allowed nearly everyone to believe that the future would be more prosperous than the present. It was this promise that softened antagonisms, made capitalism acceptable, and neutralized the idea that extreme wealth might itself be a threat to democratic cohesion. But today that promise has frayed: in many countries it is no longer credible, or no longer credible for the majority. The perception of injustice has crossed the psychological threshold beyond which order is no longer seen as imperfect but as illegitimate.

In this context, elites understand that the demand for tax justice is not an ideological fad: it is the symptom of a deep tension. It signals that society no longer believes the narrative that justified inequalities as temporary, functional, or deserved. When this belief fades, inequality itself changes nature: it is no longer an economic fact but a political one. It becomes a threat to stability, a potential call for radical transformation. This is where progressive taxation—accepted or even invoked by elites—enters as a tool of prevention. Paying more is not a concession; it is an act of preventive maintenance. It is the equivalent of lowering the pressure in a boiler that is about to explode.

Elites do not fear the poverty of the many; they fear its politicization. They fear that hardship may turn into mobilization, that discontent may become a demand, that the perception of injustice may crystallize into a call for restructuring power. This possibility—more psychological than material, more cultural than economic—is the true blind spot of stability. Money can buy many things, but it cannot buy the erasure of inequality when inequality becomes too visible, too daily, too unbearable. Hence the urgency to offer signals: look, we are not indifferent; look, the system knows how to correct itself; look, wealth is responsible. These signals do not change the structure of injustice, but they change how injustice is perceived. And this, for the preservation of order, is far more important than real justice.

Preventing the collapse of the social contract therefore means preventing inequality from entering the realm of politics. Economic inequality is tolerable; politicized inequality is explosive. The taxation accepted by elites aims precisely to avoid this politicization: it offers society a small immediate sacrifice to avert a potentially devastating transformation. It is the equivalent of reinforcing a dam not because it is already collapsing but because one has noticed that the water has changed color, pressure, smell. It is an intelligence of danger, not a generosity of heart.

The paradox is that this gesture, though presented as an ethical act, has the exact structure of self-preservation. Elites are not trying to rescue the many; they are trying to prevent the many from ceasing to believe in the legitimacy of the few. It is a sophisticated form of anticipatory defense, a symbolic vaccine administered to society to prevent a political epidemic. Taxation, in this sense, is not a withdrawal; it is a promise—the promise that the system is not abandoned to itself, that it is not pure arbitrariness, that it still contains a margin of fairness. It is a promise that elites know is partial, but sufficient. And above all, they know that without that promise, the social contract would crack to the point of no return.

The Fiscal Globalization

OECD, G20, BEPS, MINIMUM TAX

When public debate turns to taxing the rich, it still imagines a national conflict: a government that decides, a parliament that votes, an economic elite that either accepts or resists. But this image belongs to the past. Tax policy has long ceased to be an internal matter of states; it has become a field negotiated, coordinated, and in large part defined by supranational bodies whose stated task is to limit tax avoidance—and whose unstated task is to make the global ecosystem of capital predictable and stable. In this landscape, acronyms like OECD, G20, BEPS, and minimum tax are not mere technicalities: they are the names of the new architecture of fiscal power. And understanding how they function means understanding why global elites prefer taxation that is uniform, centralized, and international over taxation that is national, conflictual, and unpredictable.

The OECD, an organization born to coordinate postwar economic policy, has slowly transformed itself into the normative workshop of global capitalism. It does not govern states, but it governs the rules by which states may govern. In the fiscal realm, its role has become crucial: it builds principles, harmonizes definitions, determines what a country may or may not do to attract capital, and identifies which practices are "unacceptable" in the new international order. The OECD does not levy taxes; it makes certain forms of taxation possible or impossible. And it is precisely in this kind of power—normative, discreet, pervasive—that elites find an ally: a global referee ensuring that no state can suddenly rebel against market logic by imposing punitive taxes that would drive capital away. Here, "tax justice" is not a moral choice but a code of behavior designed to prevent destructive tax wars.

The G20, for its part, represents the political face of this new fiscal power. Born in response to financial crises, it has become the table where major economies agree on the frameworks within which smaller states will then have to operate. The decisive point is that the G20 speaks a language that does not belong to parliaments: it speaks of stability, predictability, efficiency, cooperation. It is a language that affirms a silent principle: taxation must serve the functioning of the global system, not the democratic will of individual countries. When the G20 declares that the rich and multinational corporations must "pay their fair share," it is not opening the door to a genuine redistributive conflict; it is pre-empting, with strategic foresight, a political pressure that could otherwise escape control. It transforms a demand for justice into a technical reform, a threat into a multilateral agreement, a potential social clash into regulatory codification.

The BEPS project (Base Erosion and Profit Shifting) is the most sophisticated version of this process: a vast operation of normative engineering officially aimed at preventing multinationals from artificially shifting profits to tax havens. BEPS, however, has a second, less explicit purpose: to create a unified fiscal grammar that makes corporate behavior predictable and integrated into a global order. The current system—built on fiscal residence, transfer pricing, and profit allocation criteria—is not only an attempt to limit avoidance; it is a way of making unilateral deviations by states impossible, or at least ineffective. It is no longer the state that defines the tax base; it is the international ecosystem that defines what the state may tax. What remains for states is implementation, not invention. Taxation thus becomes a form of delegated sovereignty.

The culmination of this process is the global minimum tax, the 15% levy on multinational enterprises. Presented as a progressive revolution—and indeed hailed as such by many observers—it once again represents a double movement: it closes certain loopholes, but opens a new regime of supranational discipline. Its real logic is not to penalize multinationals, which can largely internalize its cost; it is to prevent states from using tax competition as an instrument of autonomous economic policy. The minimum tax, in short, is not a means to strengthen states but to contain them: it prevents them from competing by lowering taxes, but also prevents them from competing by raising taxes unpredictably. It stabilizes a global playing field in which, ultimately, the very economic actors who are ostensibly being "taxed" remain the primary beneficiaries of predictability.

For global elites, the uniformization of taxation is not a risk—it is a safeguard. It ensures that no state, under pressure from its own public opinion, can suddenly enact radical measures; that no internal political crisis can turn into a destabilizing economic experiment; that taxation is calculable, negotiated, mediated through institutions that speak a language compatible with the interests of capital. And above all, it ensures that the call to "tax the rich" is absorbed and neutralized in the least threatening form possible: a global reform, coordinated, distant from public squares, devoid of direct conflict, administered by technical bodies.

This is the true fiscal globalization: not the end of tax avoidance, but the end of fiscal policy as a site of social struggle. Not the increase of justice, but the increase of stability. A world in which the rich accept being taxed is a world in which taxation has become a technology of global governance, not a tool of redistribution. A world in which injustice is not eliminated but regulated. A world in which sovereignty does not disappear but is redirected toward the more modest—and safer—task of implementing decisions taken elsewhere. And in this world, elites are not the victims of taxation; they are its architects and its first beneficiaries.

HOW STATE SOVEREIGNTY IS HOLLOWED OUT

Fiscal globalization is not merely a set of technical rules that coordinate international taxation: it is a process of progressive hollowing-out of state sovereignty—one that occurs not through an act of force, but through a voluntary, slow, almost imperceptible delegation made necessary by the complexity of the contemporary world. States do not abandon their power; they relinquish it out of exhaustion, impotence, convenience, or to avoid consequences they can no longer control. The result is not the abolition of sovereignty but its transformation into an administrative role: the state does not decide, it applies; it does not imagine, it executes; it does not define the economic framework, it manages it within boundaries set by others.

The first mechanism through which sovereignty is hollowed out is the loss of the ability to define autonomously what is taxable. Once, the tax base was an internal matter: the parliament decided what to tax and how. Today, the very definitions of "profit," "transfer pricing," "tax residence," and "significant economic activity" are governed by international standards. National fiscal concepts no longer exist; what exist are national interpretations of global concepts. This means that the state no longer controls the conceptual foundations of its own tax system: it can move only within the semantics established by supranational bodies. When a country attempts to redefine one of these categories—by imposing, for example, an autonomous digital tax—the international reaction is immediate and disciplining: the threat is no longer merely economic but geopolitical.

The implicit message is simple: conceptual sovereignty is no longer yours.

The second mechanism is dependence on capital flows. In a globalized economy, taxation cannot be decided without considering the reaction of markets. Governments are forced to ask not how much would be fair to tax, but what effects taxation will have on capital movements, investor confidence, and the placement of public debt. Here, the state's freedom is limited not by a treaty but by a systemic constraint: if it decides "too autonomously," capital moves elsewhere. It is a conditional sovereignty, one that exists only insofar as it does not clash with the logic of transnational financial flows. The state can be sovereign over what does not interest capital; over everything else, it is compelled to negotiate.

The third mechanism is regulatory harmonization. Tax rules are increasingly less political instruments and increasingly technical requirements. They are not designed to express a vision of society but to avoid distortions in the global market. In this framework, the state loses the political use of taxation: it can no longer employ it to redistribute, to direct development, to correct internal inequalities. It can only adapt to a set of rules that privilege neutrality over democratic will. This neutralization is presented as progress—less arbitrariness, more coherence—but in reality it is the contemporary form of depoliticization: anything that could become a site of conflict is transformed into a technical matter. And what is technical cannot be contested, nor genuinely negotiated.

The fourth mechanism, deeper and less visible, is the displacement of decision-making power. The place where tax policy is decided is no longer the state but the informal spaces of dialogue between political and technocratic elites: restricted councils, committees, working groups, bodies without direct democratic accountability. The state participates, but it does not dominate. It is one actor among many—often one of the weakest. Power shifts toward those who can control the global narrative, manage technical complexity, and represent the interest of "the system" rather than that of the population. This is not a conspiracy; it is a functional evolution. States delegate because they no longer know how to govern taxation autonomously; they delegate because avoiding chaos appears more important than preserving sovereignty.

Finally, the fifth mechanism is the progressive internalization by states of the very language of economic power. When governments speak of tax competitiveness, investment attractiveness, market stability, they are already speaking within the grammar that constrains them. This internalization is not merely theoretical; it is psychological. The state no longer thinks as a sovereign subject but as a manager of favorable conditions. Political will is replaced by the administration of the existing. And when political will disappears, sovereignty is already lost—even without anyone having formally taken it away.

In this process, taxing the rich becomes a highly symbolic gesture: it shows that the state "reacts," "restores order," "delivers justice." But this justice is granted only within the boundaries that the new fiscal order allows. It is not the state imposing its vision; it is the global system granting the state a narrow margin of action, provided it does not challenge its fundamental rules. Progressive taxation thus becomes a ritual: an act that appears sovereign but that unfolds entirely under external conditions. The citizen sees the state taxing the rich; the rich see the state performing a script.

Sovereignty is not emptied with a single blow; it is emptied when the state, though acting, always acts within frameworks it did not choose. When taxation becomes global, fiscal policy becomes local. And when politics becomes local, democracy becomes administration. Elites, in this scenario, are not hostile to the state: they need a state that functions—but that does not decide. A state that guarantees legality, not justice; stability, not equality. A state that is no longer the architect of order but its custodian. And global taxation is the most effective—and the most discreet—way to keep it in this position.

Taxing the Rich Increases Their Power

THE "INDISPENSABLE DONORS" EFFECT

When a society decides—or believes it decides—that the rich should contribute more to the funding of public functions, it imagines that it is taking power away from those who have too much of it. In reality, under the way progressive taxation is conceived and practiced today, the opposite often occurs: the more fiscal systems depend on large taxpayers, the more indispensable those taxpayers become to the functioning of the state. This is the deep paradox of modern fiscality: the act meant to limit the power of the rich ends up consolidating it.

The mechanism through which this happens can be called the "indispensable donors" effect. Any system that concentrates a significant share of its tax revenue on a narrow economic elite inevitably exposes itself to a form of dependence: the state becomes vulnerable to the possibility that these actors—individuals or corporations—might reorganize their activities, move their capital, reduce their taxable base, change jurisdiction, or simply not cooperate as expected. Even without any intention to exert pressure, even without a single explicit threat, the very structure of the fiscal system creates an asymmetrical relationship: the state needs the rich far more than the rich need the state. It is not a political relationship; it is a structural one.

The most immediate outcome is that the taxed elite becomes the consulted elite. When a government depends significantly on the fiscal contribution of the wealthy, it can no longer treat them as passive objects of policy; it must treat them as partners. Tax reforms, in this context, inevitably become negotiated: they are no longer conceived as instruments through which the state imposes a vision of society, but as bargaining processes between public interest and private tolerability. Major taxpayers, consciously or not, acquire an informal veto right: not because they explicitly exercise it, but because the entire system fears the consequences of their potential disaffection. A democracy that survives on the hope that the top 0.1% will not lose confidence is already a vulnerable democracy.

To this is added a second layer of power, even more penetrating and less perceived: the narrative. When the rich are presented as those who "hold up public finances," "pay more than anyone," "keep the state running," a cultural image is constructed that turns them into benefactors—even when they are simply paying what they owe. This image grants them additional moral legitimacy: they are not only wealthy, but useful; not only privileged, but necessary; not only few, but indispensable. A society that internalizes this idea can no longer conceive of radical redistribution: it would be interpreted not as an act of justice but as an act of self-harm. The rich thus become the secular equivalent of "major donors" in charitable institutions: figures who cannot be alienated because their contribution is deemed vital.

The third element concerns the way fiscal dependence reshapes political mentality. Governments accustomed to thinking in terms of budget constraints come to regard the wealthiest taxpayers as resources to protect, not actors to regulate. A kind of inverted paternalism emerges: it is no longer the rich who fear the state, but the state that fears the rich. From this comes the caution with which many governments approach wealth taxation: loudly invoked, quietly diluted, symbolically progressive, rarely incisive. Public fiscal power is thus diminished not by explicit opposition from the rich but by the implicit awareness that it cannot afford to lose even a portion of their contribution. In other words: the fiscal instrument meant to rebalance power ends up producing a power that is even harder to contest.

There is also a fourth effect, more cultural than economic: the personalization of wealth. When tax revenue depends significantly on a small group of individuals, media and public attention turn those taxpayers into public figures. They become "the faces" of fiscal contribution, the people who "pay for everyone." This produces a symbolic paradox: wealth, usually seen as a privilege, becomes a form of public service. The elite not only accumulate—they sustain society. And in this seemingly generous gesture lies one of the deepest shifts in contemporary power: the transformation of wealthy actors into moral agents of the common good, whose presence is perceived as a condition of stability.

Finally, the fifth element: the deterrence effect. When a society depends on the rich, even the hypothetical possibility that the rich may "leave" becomes a political argument. It is a silent blackmail that no one needs to articulate. Every fiscal debate is haunted by the implicit question: how far can we go before they go elsewhere? It is a question that defines the limits of democratic sovereignty: what is formally decidable is no longer politically feasible. At that point, power is exercised not only through actual capital but through its potential mobility.

The "indispensable donors" effect thus creates a vicious circle: the more the state relies on concentrated wealth, the more it must protect that wealth; the more it protects it, the more central that wealth becomes; the more central it becomes, the more the elite acquires a political role without passing through any democratic legitimation. Taxing the rich, in this sense, does not reduce power: it structures it, makes it organic to the political order, integrates it as a necessary element. And what is necessary cannot be opposed—only administered.

WHY MORE TAXES = MORE INFLUENCE

The idea that taxing the rich more heavily reduces their influence is intuitive, reassuring, and politically marketable. But in the reality of complex systems, the opposite often occurs: the more an elite contributes to the financing of the collective order, the more voice, weight, recognition, and political leverage it acquires. Taxation—when it is not confiscatory and does not arise from a radical conflict—becomes the mechanism through which wealth is integrated into the heart of the state, transforming itself from a regulated actor into a regulating one. Financial participation becomes political participation; contribution becomes power.

The first reason is structural: those who finance a significant share of the state automatically become privileged interlocutors of that state. This dynamic is as old as fiscal societies themselves, but today it takes on a new, refined, almost invisible form. If a substantial portion of public revenue depends on a very wealthy minority, the government cannot treat that minority as a mere taxpayer; it must treat it as a strategic partner, or risk destabilizing its fiscal base. This partnership is never formalized—it would be scandalous if it were—but it is so evident at a systemic level that it conditions public action. Democracy no longer speaks only to its citizens; it speaks also, and above all, to its key taxpayers.

The second reason concerns the way progressive taxation ennobles the role of the rich. The elite who publicly accept paying more appear, in the eyes of society, as responsible, farsighted actors capable of looking beyond their immediate self-interest. This grants them a particularly valuable form of power: moral power. When a dominant group manages to present its advantages as a service rendered to the community—"we pay more than anyone, we support the state, we fund public services"—its influence becomes doubly difficult to contest. Those who pay have a voice; those who pay a great deal have a great voice. And those who have a great voice, in a society that has increasingly delegated its political imagination to private actors, inevitably end up shaping public discourse.

The third reason is the professionalization of elite political participation. Modern great fortunes are not just accumulated wealth; they are fully fledged organizational apparatuses, equipped with foundations, lobbying offices, research centers, academic networks, think tanks. These instruments do not operate *despite* taxation but *because* of it. The more their contribution to the fiscal system grows, the more they can legitimize—both to governments and to the public—their presence in decision-making processes. It is the transformation of the rich into experts: those who pay are also those who understand; those who understand become those who advise; and those who advise, in contemporary politics, are often those who decide. The public sphere is thus filled with authoritative voices speaking in the name of fiscal sustainability, responsibility, and balanced budgets: rhetorics that function as carriers of private influence.

The fourth reason, more subtle, is psychological: taxation creates a symbolic right to participate. If the average citizen perceives the state as a distant, bureaucratic entity, the elite who contribute massively perceive it as a structure partly their own. Not because they own it, but because they sustain it. The relationship is no longer vertical—the state imposes, the rich obey—but horizontal: the state and the wealthy co-govern the functioning of social order. When fiscal reforms, public investments, or industrial policies are discussed, major taxpayers do not perceive themselves as subjects of the decision; they perceive themselves as part of the entity that decides. And this perception—whether shared by society or not—translates into real influence, because it manifests precisely in the places where power is actually exercised.

The fifth reason is what might be called the "room at the top" effect. When taxing the rich becomes a central topic, the elites are not forced to defend themselves; they are invited to participate. Every fiscal reform demands their presence, their opinion, their consent. More taxes mean more technical committees, more consultations, more conferences, more public interventions. Their voice, far from being marginalized, is amplified. Society, in attempting to discipline wealth, ends up giving it a larger microphone. It is a circular dynamic: the elite appear necessary because they contribute; and by contributing, they become indispensable in shaping the conditions of their own contribution.

The ultimate result is a reversal that many fail to see: taxing the rich does not reduce the power of the wealthy class—rather, it makes that power a structural co-management of the state. An elite that takes on an ever-greater share of the fiscal burden becomes a kind of guarantor of the system, a custodian of its continuity. Its influence no longer rests solely on the capital it owns, but on the capital it mobilizes for the functioning of the state. Not on wealth held, but on wealth deployed. It is a power that does not impose itself *against* the state but that articulates itself *within* the state; it does not weaken institutions but permeates them. And because it appears legitimate, responsible, even generous, it becomes harder to contest than any historical form of elite power.

In such a world, more taxes do not mean less power. They mean a different kind of power: more discreet, more capillary, more integrated, more protected. A power that cloaks itself in the morality of sacrifice to strengthen the solidity of its position. And that, behind the façade of fiscal justice, achieves the most sophisticated form of political influence democracies have ever known.

PART III
POWER

The Hollowing Out of the State

FROM STATE SOVEREIGNTY TO PRIVATE GOVERNANCE

The shift from state sovereignty to private governance is neither a silent coup nor a conspiracy: it is an organic process born from the widening gap between the complexity of the contemporary world and the capacity of states to govern it. When an institutional power can no longer control the flows, actors, technologies, and infrastructures that define collective reality, it does not formally abdicate; it is simply bypassed. A new space emerges—a nameless territory—in which states continue to exist, but no longer as ordering principles: they exist as local administrators of an ecosystem whose decision-making centers lie elsewhere. It is in this space that what we call *private governance* thrives: a set of non-state actors who, despite lacking political authority in the traditional sense, exercise functions that once belonged exclusively to states.

The deeper reason for this shift is that modern sovereignty, as conceived since the seventeenth century, was designed for a closed, territorial, slow world. The sovereign state could control borders, discipline the domestic economy, impose rules within its territory, and defend it from external interference. But that world is gone. Today borders are permeable to flows of capital, data, digital services, information, and logistics. Wealth no longer accumulates in physical spaces: it moves through private infrastructures, servers, platforms, global networks that no state fully controls. The real economy depends on infrastructures owned by private actors; political communication takes place on private platforms; states' cybersecurity lies in the hands of private companies; even the functioning of democracy depends on algorithms that no public institution designed. Under these conditions, the old idea of sovereignty does not disappear—it simply becomes insufficient.

Private governance emerges precisely in the gap between what the state *should* do and what it is no longer able to do. Global corporations—only those equipped with infrastructural power—not only produce goods or services: they set standards, arbitrate disputes, define protocols, regulate entire segments of social life. In the world of platforms, for instance, public authority arrives second. It is not the state that decides how digital space must be structured: platforms impose architectures, modes of communication, rules of conduct, visibility criteria, algorithms that shape public opinion. The state steps in only when these architectures are already stabilized—and often cannot modify them even then. In this sense, private governance is not mere influence: it is the production of order.

The same applies to the economic sphere. Global flows are not regulated by states but by international standards, technical codes, banking networks, payment systems, and multilateral agreements. Corporations operating in this ecosystem are no longer regulated subjects: they are decision nodes. They can choose jurisdictions, dictate terms, negotiate tax arrangements, threaten relocations. Their power is not coercive in the classical sense—it is structural. They act as sovereigns without needing to declare it, simply because states can no longer do without them. Their influence does not derive from the possession of force but from the possession of infrastructure. And whoever controls infrastructure, in the modern world, holds what used to constitute sovereignty: the capacity to make certain actions possible or impossible.

The hollowing out of the state does not mean that private power replaces the state, but that it flows through it. Private governance operates as a network of decisions that moves around the state, not against it. It does not seek to overthrow democratic institutions: it leaves them intact, provided they do not interfere with the systemic logics it organizes. In many cases, states themselves resort to private governance to compensate for their own incapacity: they sign agreements with digital platforms to manage public communication; delegate security functions to tech firms; outsource energy, logistics, and digital infrastructure to entities they cannot control. Each delegation produces a further weakening, and each weakening produces new delegation. Thus, without noise, a parallel sovereignty takes shape.

Private governance is not illegitimate because it is private; it is illegitimate because it cannot be contested through traditional means. Against a state, a citizen can appeal to the law, public opinion, or political institutions. Against a global platform or a multinational corporation, they have no equivalent tools. Private governance is not politically accountable because it is not formally political, yet it exercises political power in every substantive sense: it determines what we can do, see, say, buy, or transfer. In this sense, it does not abolish state sovereignty: it renders it decorative. The state retains faces, symbols, rituals, and apparatuses; but the material conditions that make its action possible are articulated elsewhere.

This is not a process that can be reversed with a legislative act, because it does not arise from a deliberate decision by elites, but from a deep transformation in the relationship between economy, technology, and politics. The nation-state is an artifact of the industrial world; private governance is the natural expression of the networked world. And in this transition we understand why taxing the rich does not reduce the power of the global elite: it transfers, distributes, and integrates it into a system no longer measurable in terms of borders but in terms of infrastructures. Private governance does not hollow out the state because it is stronger than the state, but because the state has ceased to be the place where the world is organized.

The result is an order in which the formal sovereignty of states coexists with the effective sovereignty of actors with no territorial anchoring, no citizenry to answer to, and no electoral accountability. This is the new geography of power: a map in which borders still exist, but no longer demarcate the space of decision-making. And in which private wealth, far from being disciplined by the state, becomes one of the primary gears of the machine that has taken its place.

THE ROLE OF GLOBAL PLATFORMS

Global platforms are today the most advanced laboratory of the transformation of political power into infrastructural power. They are not merely technology companies: they are environments in which an ever-growing portion of social, economic, cultural, and even emotional life takes place. They have replaced the public sphere without ever declaring it, and they have done so not by offering ideas but by offering *functions*. In a world where nearly every activity—communicating, working, purchasing, informing oneself, storing data, voting, traveling—passes through private infrastructures, the platform is not a market actor: it is the *terrain* on which the market itself unfolds. And whoever controls the terrain is no longer regulated by sovereignty; sovereignty, rather, must negotiate its access to that terrain.

The most revolutionary aspect of platforms is that they are private spaces with public effects. What happens within them is never neutral: it shapes opinions, behaviors, consumption patterns, forms of relationship, local and global economies, information cycles, and political dynamics. And yet no state has anything close to comparable control over these spaces. Crucial decisions—what content to make visible, what to hide, which activities to privilege, which flows to incentivize or disincentivize, which interactions to make possible or impossible—are not taken in parliaments but by internal policy teams, by algorithms trained on proprietary criteria, by boards of directors accountable not to citizens but to shareholders. The state may impose certain limits, but it cannot govern the overall architecture of the system. And when you do not control the architecture, you do not control what becomes reality within that architecture.

The power of platforms does not lie primarily in their financial scale—though it is enormous—but in the fact that they function as the obligatory interface between individuals and the world. States can still legislate, but platforms define the concrete ways in which those laws translate into experience. The algorithm that determines the visibility of a news item weighs more than the law on freedom of the press; the recommendation system that guides consumption weighs more than industrial policy; the cybersecurity protocols adopted by a major tech company weigh more than national cybersecurity strategies. States continue to speak the language of sovereignty, while platforms speak the language of *actuality*. And actuality always prevails.

This asymmetry produces a profound effect: states become actors that must negotiate with platforms what they once would simply have decided. It is a cultural shift before it is a political one. Public institutions, to function, must often rely on private infrastructures: to communicate with citizens, to collect data, to manage essential services, to monitor flows of information. But every reliance is a dependency. Platforms therefore become co-governors, not because they claim the role, but because the state can no longer do without them. No government today can remain entirely outside digital ecosystems, just as no citizen can live outside networks of connection. The platform is the new natural habitat of human action. And what is natural no longer needs to justify itself.

Their power grows further because they do not operate within territorial boundaries. They are extrajurisdictional actors: their legal headquarters is irrelevant compared to the material reach of their power. This allows them to escape any attempt at national containment. If a state imposes overly stringent regulations, a platform can redirect its services elsewhere, negotiate terms, invoke unsustainable costs, or mobilize international pressure. In practice, it exercises sovereignty through mobility: it does not need to oppose states head-on; it merely needs to be able to relocate its strategic nodes. States, by contrast, cannot move. And in the conflict between what is mobile and what is immobile, the mobile always wins.

Perhaps the most significant aspect is that platforms have redefined the very notion of citizenship without ever naming it. The contemporary individual is, above all, a user; and the user obeys rules that have no democratic foundation, require no public legitimacy, and can change at any moment without consultation. Digital citizenship, *de facto*, is governed by the platform; political citizenship, *de jure*, by the state. But the former increasingly determines how the latter can be exercised. A society that lives inside platforms implicitly accepts their authority because it lacks functional alternatives. And authority accepted for lack of alternatives is the most stable form of power.

For these reasons, global platforms are the clearest—and the hardest to challenge—example of how private governance has overtaken state sovereignty. They do not seek to assume the role of the state: they assume control of the conditions that make the state's action possible. They do not replace politics: they set the framework within which politics can still exist. They do not dominate citizens: they define the environment in which citizens move and think. It is a form of power that does not need to impose itself because it coincides with the infrastructure everyone uses, the time everyone inhabits, the everyday gestures no one perceives as political anymore. Their dominion is invisible because it has already become natural.

In this new order, speaking of "state sovereignty" remains possible only in a formal sense. The substance lies elsewhere: in the hands of those who control the networks. And unless states learn to reinvent themselves as builders of infrastructures, not merely producers of rules, private governance will continue to grow—silently but inexorably.

THE NEW TECHNOCRATIC MODEL

The rise of private governance does not merely weaken the state: it produces a new form of government, a paradigm no longer grounded in political representation, democratic conflict, or institutional mediation, but in technical competence embedded in opaque infrastructures and in decisions made *before* politics. The technocracy of the past—of ministries, central banks, and planning agencies—still appeared as an extension of the state: technicians applying a political vision. The new technocratic model does not apply a political vision; it *replaces* it. It does not govern in the name of a project, but in the name of a complexity it declares ungovernable by traditional tools. It is a technocracy no longer state-based but systemic: a form of power that legitimizes itself through its own indispensability.

Its fundamental characteristic is that it never presents itself as power. Technical authority does not wear the face of command: it wears the face of inevitability. Decisions are not imposed; they emerge as the natural result of analyses, predictive models, simulations, international best practices. Politics no longer decides what must be done: it ratifies what "cannot be otherwise." Technique becomes a metaphysics of order: what works is what is true; what is true is what is necessary; what is necessary is what must be done. Political freedom dissolves within this sequence, because no decision is truly chosen: it is always a response to conditions presented as indisputable.

The new technocratic model is born here: in the transformation of emergency into normality. Every domain becomes too complex to be left to democratic deliberation: global taxation, platform regulation, digital security, energy transition, financial flows. In each of these fields, states recognize in themselves a kind of structural incompetence. And when a power acknowledges its own incompetence, technique presents itself as the only rational voice. Decisions are no longer made by those who represent the popular will, but by those who interpret data. And data, in turn, do not represent the world: they construct it, select it, and render it governable according to criteria that the population neither defines nor can verify.

This technocracy no longer operates in the classical form of "advising the rulers," because it eliminates the distinction between advisor and ruler. The technician does not support the political decision; he *replaces* it. Major platforms, infrastructural corporations, supranational agencies, central banks operate as actors who see farther, faster, and more globally than any government—not only because of analytical capacity, but because they possess the information that defines the field of possible action. In this schema, states become recipients of reports, recommendations, standards, and guidelines. And whoever controls the standard controls the behavior of states more than a state can control the behavior of a citizen.

The most unsettling feature of the new technocratic model is its non-conflictual nature. Politics, by definition, lives from conflict: competing interests, values, and visions of the world collide and eventually find compromise. Technocracy, instead, eliminates conflict by declaring it irrational. What is not aligned with technical criteria is presented as dangerous, incompetent, populist. There is no longer confrontation between alternatives, because technique admits no alternatives: only more or less efficient solutions. Democracy is not abolished; it is hollowed out. Elections continue, parliaments continue, governments succeed one another, but the real space of decision shrinks into a narrow corridor policed by technical constraints no one has voted for.

In this logic, the nation-state does not die: it becomes an office for implementing directives originating from international bodies, expert groups, digital platforms, and networks of private standards. And technocracy does not merely advise the state: it penetrates it. It provides the data, the infrastructures, the modelling tools, the operational platforms. In short: it provides the very capacity to govern. But whatever grants capacity also generates dependence. Once a technical infrastructure is adopted, a state loses the ability to govern without it. Technocracy thus becomes the natural environment of public action: the entity that defines what is possible, what is reasonable, what is necessary. And whoever defines what is possible governs more than whoever signs the decree.

The new technocratic model is not the end of the state, but the end of its centrality. The state remains the official face of power, while beneath the surface operate the mechanisms that guide it, surpass it, anticipate it. Technocracy does not seek visibility: it seeks to be recognized as obvious. And when power becomes obvious, it becomes untranslatable into the language of politics.

The Great Compensation

HOW A NEW MORAL LEGITIMACY IS BUILT

The great compensation begins the moment elites realize that their material power can no longer be justified through the traditional narrative of merit, nor through the now-hollow promises of shared progress. When a society no longer believes that wealth is the sign of extraordinary talent or of a service rendered to the community, wealth itself becomes fragile—not materially fragile, but symbolically exposed, stripped of that aura of inevitability that has protected it for centuries. It is into this void that moral compensation emerges: a process through which economic power re-legitimizes its existence not by reducing inequality, but by producing around it a new ethical framework.

The starting point is simple: when power can no longer be justified by the past, it must be justified by the future. If wealth is no longer the reward for individual success, it must become the instrument through which collective problems are solved. This is how elites begin to present themselves not as beneficiaries of the system, but as its custodians—its only actors capable of addressing challenges the state can no longer manage on its own: ecological transition, digitalization, cybersecurity, climate mitigation, technological innovation, the governance of global flows. Wealth loses its aristocratic aura and acquires a messianic one. No longer *I possess because I merit*, but *I possess because I must lead*. It is a silent, yet radical mutation.

The second movement of the great compensation is the transformation of economic contribution into civic virtue. It does not matter whether an additional tax paid by a billionaire has a marginal effect on his fortune; what matters is that the gesture can be narrated as proof of responsibility. Societies need symbols more than figures, and power knows this. That is why moral legitimacy is not built on actual redistribution, but on the *representation* of redistribution: public statements, collective appeals, declarations in support of tax reforms, conferences in which major business leaders call for more justice, strategic philanthropy, ethical investments, foundations "for the common good." Morality, in this context, is not an inner quality; it is a performative language. Goodness is not practiced; it is staged. And staging—in the contemporary world—counts as much as, and often more than, practice.

The third component of compensation is the neutralization of conflict. A deeply unequal society should be traversed by radical tensions; and yet it is not. Why? Because the moral legitimacy constructed by elites turns inequality into a "complex" issue—one that cannot be resolved by political conflict but only through the responsible guidance of those who already hold power. The message is subtle but powerful: injustices are not to be eliminated; they are to be managed. And not by politics, but by those who possess the technical, financial, and infrastructural tools to do so. The rich, once antagonists, become guarantors. Elites, once the problem, become the solution. Conflict, once a democratic dynamic, becomes a misunderstanding.

The fourth element is the production of a new ethics of vulnerability. Contemporary elites present themselves as exposed, unprotected subjects: exposed to global risks, financial crises, technological disruptions, geopolitical threats. In this narrative, their wealth no longer appears as a shield but as a burden, a responsibility, a task. The idea spreads that the rich are themselves victims of complexity, forced to navigate an ungovernable world, and that their privileged position makes them *more capable*—not more culpable—of managing that complexity. It is a refined way of transforming material superiority into a form of moral fragility. And when even the rich appear fragile, conflict fades: who would attack the vulnerable?

The fifth movement of the great compensation is the construction of selective moral communities. Through donations, cultural projects, civic initiatives, elites build around themselves microcosms of recognized virtue: universities, museums, foundations, educational programs, innovation hubs, "ethical" businesses. These spaces do not serve to correct inequality; they serve to reinterpret it. The elite appear as generators of civic value, not concentrators of private value. Whoever controls the cultural imagination controls society's moral judgment. And whoever controls moral judgment no longer needs to justify their wealth: its justification is supplied by others.

Finally, the great compensation reaches its peak when morality becomes the ultimate form of sovereignty. The state no longer holds the monopoly on legitimacy; it shares it with private actors who have succeeded in building for themselves a superior ethical reputation. Elites become the moral arbiters of the system: those who determine which investments are "good," which innovations are "just," which behaviors are "responsible," which policies are "sustainable." This is an enormous power precisely because it does not appear as power: it appears as conscience, prudence, foresight. Submission arises not from force, but from trust.

This is how the new moral legitimacy is built: not by eliminating inequality, but by saturating it with ethics; not by reducing the power of elites, but by transforming that power into guidance; not by strengthening politics, but by making it dependent on a good that only private power can embody. Society is not pacified through justice; it is pacified through the *narrative* of justice. This is the great compensation: the symbolic gesture that replaces real change, morality that substitutes for equality, appearance that becomes substance. The world remains unequal, but it no longer appears unjust. And for those who hold power, that is all that matters.

PHILANTHROPY AS SOFT POWER

Contemporary philanthropy is no longer a gesture of generosity: it is a power device. It produces not only material benefits but, above all, meanings, narratives, and moral hierarchies. In a world where the political legitimacy of states is wavering, philanthropy becomes the instrument through which private elites carve out for themselves a quasi-institutional role—an authority that does not derive from democratic mandate, but from their ability to embody universally recognized values: education, health, culture, innovation, the fight against poverty. Philanthropic soft power is not the alternative to private governance; it is its luminous face, its moral aesthetic, its seductive language. And it is precisely this luminosity that makes it so powerful.

The first feature of philanthropic soft power is that it operates where the state fails. Its effectiveness arises from the crisis of public institutions: inadequate hospitals, declining schools, underfunded scientific research, an eroded welfare state. Into this void philanthropy enters as salvation, as the capacity to do what the state cannot or will not do. But every salvation creates dependence. Society learns to look to private actors as the true guarantors of essential goods. And once this dependence stabilizes, the donor is no longer perceived as one actor among many, but as a pillar of the system. Elites become indispensable not because of their wealth, but because of the services that replace public functions. This replacement is not experienced as a subtraction, but as a gift. And what is perceived as a gift cannot be contested.

The second feature is philanthropy's ability to produce cultural legitimacy. A foundation that finances museums, universities, scientific and artistic projects does more than distribute resources: it distributes prestige. It creates an aura around the benefactor's name—an aura that absolves more effectively than charity and covers more effectively than justice. Culture, by its nature, is one of the domains most difficult to criticize publicly: no one wants to appear ungrateful toward those who support art or research. This transforms philanthropy into a kind of moral shield: regardless of how great a donor's economic power may be, that power appears compensated by a contribution to society's intellectual heritage. In this sense, philanthropic soft power surpasses propaganda: it does not persuade, it educates. It does not convince, it shapes.

The third element is its capacity to shape the public agenda. Philanthropic foundations do not merely distribute funds: they select causes, identify problems, define priorities, introduce concepts, establish what is "important" and what is not. A society in which scientific research, education, or innovation depend on private funding is a society in which private actors decide what is worthy of being studied, taught, or developed. The state retains formal sovereignty; philanthropy exercises substantive sovereignty: it determines the content of the future. It re-harmonizes public ethics according to its own criteria, pushing themes, values, and perspectives that serve to consolidate its role. It is an agenda that appears altruistic but often aligns with worldviews conducive to maintaining the existing order.

The fourth feature is the power philanthropy exercises beyond its own territory. A European foundation can influence African education; an American foundation can shape Asian health policies; a technological foundation can mold the global climate agenda. No state has a comparable reach. Globalized philanthropy operates with the freedom of private actors and the authority of public ones: without borders, without elections, without accountability. It is a form of soft power that needs no justification because it presents itself as a gift; and the gift, precisely because it is "free," takes the form of destiny. When a foundation decides that a certain health reform should spread, it appears as though the world itself willed it.

The fifth element of philanthropic soft power is its capacity to absorb dissent. Philanthropic elites often fund social projects, rights campaigns, environmental initiatives, minority programs —not because they seek to subvert the social order, but because they want to ensure that dissent remains manageable. Philanthropy allows space for criticism, provided that criticism does not question the structure of power itself. It promotes symbolic, not structural, transformations. It creates listening spaces, discussion tables, social innovation labs—devices that channel, aestheticize, and neutralize potentially subversive energy. Dissent remains, but it no longer targets the core of the system. And when a form of power that might be contested becomes instead the great sponsor of dissent, it has already won.

Finally, philanthropy becomes soft power in the deepest sense: by constructing a new moral imaginary. In this imaginary, wealth is not a privilege to be defended but a resource to be shared; inequality is not a threat but a condition that makes the gift possible; power is not the problem but the solution. The rich no longer appear distant but caring; not dominant but responsible; not superfluous but necessary. Philanthropy transforms power into virtue, wealth into mission, privilege into service. It is the most sophisticated of symbolic reversals: the world continues to revolve around capital, but believes it is being sustained by generosity.

Thus philanthropy becomes the ultimate form of soft power: a power that prevails not because it imposes, but because it consoles; not because it dominates, but because it guides; not because it displays itself, but because it appears indispensable. In philanthropy, the great compensation is fulfilled: morality replaces justice, gratitude replaces conflict, the narrative of good replaces redistribution. It is the new ethic of the global elite—the art of governing without governing, of influencing without appearing, of legitimizing oneself without accountability. And for that very reason, it is one of the hardest forms of power to see—and the most impossible to contest.

THE IMPLICIT PACT: "WE PAY, BUT WE DECIDE"

At the heart of the new architecture of power lies an unwritten pact—never stated explicitly, yet unmistakably present in the system's logic: elites accept contributing to the maintenance of the collective order, but in exchange they claim the right to shape its fundamental decisions. It is the pact that transforms taxation into political participation, contribution into a right of governance, private wealth into a kind of controlling stake in the management of public affairs. And the pact is all the more effective precisely because it never appears as such. No one articulates it, and yet everyone operates according to its coordinates.

The mechanism is simple: when a fiscal system relies heavily on its wealthiest taxpayers, those taxpayers inevitably become structural pillars of the state. And what is structural cannot be treated as a passive object of political will: it must be involved, consulted, respected. The language surrounding this dynamic is always that of "responsibility," "public–private cooperation," "partnerships for the common good." But beneath this conciliatory rhetoric lies a principle as ancient as it is enduring: those who pay, rule. Not explicitly, not through coercion, but through the logic of dependence itself. A state that cannot afford to lose the contribution of its major financiers cannot afford to ignore them either.

From here the implicit pact emerges: the elite accept taxation, provided taxation never becomes the instrument through which politics can discipline wealth. They agree to "do their part," provided they can participate in defining what "their part" is. And they even agree to support the rhetoric of fiscal justice—so long as that justice never translates into a true rebalancing of power. The pact does not concern the redistribution of income; it concerns the redistribution of legitimacy. The state gains an appearance of moral strength; the elite gain decision-making authority. It is a perfect exchange because it unfolds in a gray zone into which politics no longer dares to enter.

The second movement of the pact is the shift from taxation to governance. Once elites are perceived as indispensable to the functioning of the state—because they contribute to revenue, fund services, support public initiatives, invest in infrastructure—it becomes natural for them to participate in decision-making processes. This is no longer traditional lobbying, but something deeper: a moral co-governance of the system. Major economic actors become permanent interlocutors, always present at the decisive tables, always heard at critical junctures, always consulted in defining long-term strategies. Their power is no longer based on securing exemptions or privileges; it lies in helping to shape the rules themselves. The state appears as the decision-maker; the elite as the source of the rationality that guides the decision.

The third element of the pact concerns risk management. Elites do not accept taxation in order to reduce their influence, but to reduce the systemic risk that would arise from a collapse of public consensus. They pay to prevent instability, to preserve social peace, to avoid populist backlashes that might threaten their role. It is an investment, not a sacrifice. Insurance, not surrender. Progressive taxation thus becomes a mechanism for stabilizing power, not limiting it. When the wealthy accept to pay more, they do so because they know that the cost of not paying—in terms of legitimacy, visibility, reputation—would be higher. The apparent concession is, in reality, a strategy of consolidation.

The fourth movement is symbolic. Contemporary societies, lacking grand unifying narratives, require symbols of responsibility. The elite provide these symbols in the form of tax contributions, philanthropic initiatives, and support for public causes. But every symbol has a price: the price is the recognition of their role. Society accepts that the rich have a say because it perceives them as those who "are doing their part." And once this perception takes root, the elite can exercise influence not only on economic policy but on cultural, social, and educational policy as well. They decide which ideas deserve attention, which innovations should be funded, which values must be promoted. The price of their generosity is their right to define what counts as good.

Finally, the implicit pact reaches its most refined form: the fusion of economic contribution with moral authority. Elites do not merely pay; they show that they pay. They do not simply finance; they narrate their financing as an ethical act. They do not simply participate in the state; they present themselves as guarantors of its functioning. At that point, their influence no longer derives from money but from image. They become the "responsible" segment of society, the one that understands complexity, resists populism, and shoulders collective problems. The state becomes the party that asks. Society the party that waits. The elite the party that decides.

This is the true meaning of the implicit pact: decisions are not made against those who pay. Not because they impose their will by force, but because the logic of the system makes it impossible. Taxation, far from diminishing the power of the rich, integrates it into the machinery of the state, clothes it in morality, and transforms it into necessity. It is a pact with no signature, yet with profound effects: it stabilizes the existing order, blocks alternatives, turns justice into obedience and obedience into consent.

We pay, say the elites. But we decide. And in this new moral order, no one seems to have the courage to ask why.

PART IV
THE FUTURE

Three Scenarios for the Next 20 Years

1. MINIMAL STATE AND GLOBAL GOVERNANCE

The first plausible scenario for the next twenty years is one that continues—without any visible rupture—the trajectory already underway: a state that preserves its forms, its rituals, its institutional iconography, but that gradually cedes its substantive functions to a constellation of private and supranational global actors. It is a scenario of soft continuity, without visible shocks, in which power shifts like sand through the fingers, almost without anyone truly perceiving its movement. It is the world of the minimal state—not in the classical ideological sense (lower taxes, more market), but in a new, subtler, more radical sense: the state as a vestige of power, while real power is exercised elsewhere.

In this scenario, states do not disappear: they are downsized. They continue to manage basic healthcare, education, internal security, the justice system—but increasingly as local administrators of an order defined by others. Their role resembles that of municipalities in an undeclared federation: they retain autonomy over the everyday, but must conform to the technical, fiscal, and infrastructural rules set at higher levels. National politics survives as symbolic theatre; real politics takes place in global capital flows, in the algorithmic regulation of platforms, in multilateral negotiations attended by few and voted by no one.

Global governance, in this scenario, is not a world government as imagined by the utopias or dystopias of the twentieth century. It is a fabric of standards, protocols, technical regulations, fiscal treaties, interoperability agreements—rules that define what can and cannot be done. There is no sovereign centre: there is a network of centres. The OECD, IMF, G20, WTO, technical bodies, digital platforms, infrastructural corporations, philanthropic foundations—each exercises a fragment of functional sovereignty. Politics, reduced to the capacity to coordinate these forces, is no longer leadership but permanent mediation. "Governing" becomes an exercise in alignment with an order already written.

The minimal state arises from the awareness that the world has become too large, too complex, too interdependent for any single political unit to govern it. But this awareness—one that could have given rise to a new democratic federalism—gives rise instead to a distributed technocracy without popular legitimacy. Global decisions are not made by a global people, because no global people exists: they are made by institutions that treat democracy as background noise, not as a principle.

In this scenario, taxing the rich assumes an ambiguous role: it is the symbolic gesture through which the state displays its remaining moral function, even though the real ability to discipline wealth lies in the hands of global governance. The rich, for their part, accept the fiscal contribution because they know it does not threaten their position but stabilizes it: a weak state that asks is less dangerous than a strong state that decides. Elites in such a world no longer need to capture the state: the system itself renders it marginal.

The impact on citizens' lives is twofold. On one hand, a sense of efficiency: smoother digital services, faster transactions, borders that matter less for work, research, business. On the other, a growing sense of political impotence: decisions that truly matter are neither made nor explained, but announced as necessary, inevitable, technically mandated. It is a scenario that produces stability—but a stability with the flavour of a contractual clause: a peace without participation, an order without deliberation.

Democracy, in this world, does not disappear: it becomes decorative. It continues to elect representatives, but those representatives manage only the margins, not the centre. While the centre—the beating heart of global decision-making—belongs to an arena that is not public, yet nonetheless determines the fate of the public.

This scenario is neither the most dramatic nor the most catastrophic; it is simply the most likely if nothing changes. It is the natural continuation of the present trajectory. In this vision, the future does not explode: it congeals. The world continues much as it is—only a little more efficient, a little more standardized, a little more unequal, a little more governed by no one and by everyone.

The minimal state is not the end of the state: it is the end of the illusion that the state remains the place where the world is decided. And global governance is not a unified power: it is the invisible weave that fills the space politics has abandoned.

2. FISCAL WAR AMONG GEOPOLITICAL BLOCS

The second plausible scenario for the next twenty years is not the soft continuity of the first, but its mirror opposite: not a fiscal globalization that consolidates, but a fracture of globalization itself. Multilateral cooperation—OECD, G20, BEPS, the minimum tax—may fail under the weight of geopolitical rivalries, the decline of American hegemony, the rise of China, and the growing assertiveness of regional powers. The outcome would be a fiscal war not between isolated states, but between civilizational blocs, each with its own strategy for attracting capital, its own development model, its own technological infrastructure. A war fought not with weapons, but with tax rates, data regulation, market access, investment incentives, and the manipulation of standards.

The logic is simple: when the global market fractures, capital becomes a strategic resource. And what is strategic ceases to be governed by neutral rules and becomes governed by power politics. In this scenario, major economies no longer seek a common fiscal framework; they seek to maximize their own autonomy and weaken that of their rivals. Taxation becomes a geopolitical tool, not an economic one: a means to strengthen one's bloc and destabilize others. It marks a return to the logic of spheres of influence—but with new instruments.

In such a world, the United States could abandon the idea of a global minimum tax in order to attract strategic investment in the tech-military sector, offering hyper-competitive tax conditions to firms deemed essential to national security. China could do the same, but even more directly, integrating fiscal policy with cybersecurity and data control. Europe, lacking unified sovereignty, would risk oscillating between the two models, attempting to erect regulatory barriers to protect its internal market without truly managing to retain investment and innovation. Other blocs—India, Southeast Asia, the Gulf, emerging Africa—might adopt hybrid strategies, becoming zones of arbitrage between major powers.

Fiscal war would not be limited to tax rates: it would encompass everything that creates competitive advantage:

- *Data*: who can retain it, export it, monetize it.
- *Intellectual property*: which jurisdictions best protect patents and algorithms.
- *Cybersecurity*: which states offer safer digital ecosystems.
- *Critical infrastructure*: cloud, semiconductors, energy networks, supply chains.
- *Talent attraction*: ultra-aggressive personal tax regimes designed to retain scientific and entrepreneurial elites.

Taxation would thus become only the tip of the iceberg in a much broader systemic competition. And this competition would have profound effects on domestic power structures within states.

The first effect would be a radical polarization of fiscal policy. Governments would be forced into one of two opposing strategies: either becoming selective tax havens to attract strategic capital, or raising domestic taxation to compensate for the flight of mobile wealth. Both strategies are destabilizing: the former erodes the tax base; the latter erodes social consensus. Fiscal policy would therefore become one of the most volatile fronts of geopolitics.

The second effect would be the rise of a new mobile transnational elite capable of shifting from one bloc to another, from one jurisdiction to another, exploiting asymmetries and tensions. In a fragmented world, mobile capital becomes more powerful than regulated capital. Ultra-rich individuals and hyper-technological multinationals would take on a role similar to that of merchant cities in the late Middle Ages: arbiters among rival powers, beneficiaries of every asymmetry, protagonists of a game in which states compete to attract them.

The third effect would be a deep erosion of European integration. Without common fiscal policy and without coordinated industrial strategy, Europe risks internal Balkanization: Ireland against France, the Netherlands against Germany, Italy against everyone. The divisions already simmering beneath the surface would intensify, and the EU could become a regulatory battleground between the United States and China, rather than an autonomous actor.

The fourth and perhaps most serious effect would be the destabilization of the domestic social contract. If citizens perceive that taxes rise while global capital escapes, fiscal legitimacy collapses. The question "why me, and not them?" becomes explosive. This could fuel a new generation of populist movements centered not on cultural identity, but on a radical critique of mobile economic power and of governments incapable of disciplining it.

A fiscal war among blocs does not produce a new order: it produces an ordered disorder, a permanent competition with no stable winners. In such a world, taxing the rich is no longer an act of justice nor a mechanism of moral compensation: it becomes a strategic weapon. Elites no longer ask to be taxed: they choose where to be taxed. And the state can no longer use fiscal policy to govern wealth: it can only use it in the hope of keeping wealth within its borders.

This scenario is more unstable, more conflictual, more risky than the first. But for that very reason, it is also plausible. The world does not always move toward order; often, it moves toward fracture. And in fracture, power does not disappear: it concentrates.

3. THE RETURN OF HARD ECONOMIC NATIONALISM

The third scenario does not envision the continuation of globalization nor its fracture into technocratic blocs, but the possibility— increasingly evoked, increasingly tangible— that states will attempt to reclaim the power they have lost. Not as a technical adjustment, but as an act of political force: a return of hard economic nationalism. Not the rhetorical and symbolic version we already see today— a few tariffs, a few migration restrictions, a few campaigns against multinationals— but a structural transformation of the relationship between state, market, and capital. A true reversal of direction, in which sovereignty seeks to reassert itself not through compromise, but through confrontation.

This scenario is not a nostalgic return to the 1950s: it is a leap into a future in which a multipolar and unstable world pushes states to redefine their priorities. More than ideological, it is a nationalism of necessity. Because if globalization ceases to be a circuit that produces broad-based growth and becomes an arena of permanent vulnerability, states will be tempted to protect what remains of their political margin through closure rather than openness.

The first feature of this scenario is the re-nationalization of the strategic economy. States begin to retain—by any means necessary—the decision-making centers of key industries: energy, semiconductors, digital infrastructure, payment networks, artificial intelligence, defense, advanced logistics. The goal is no longer to attract global investment, but to prevent vital decisions from being made elsewhere. The result is an aggressive industrial policy built on selective incentives, regulatory barriers, state equity stakes, partial nationalizations. The economy no longer guides politics: politics once again shapes the economy, despite the cost.

The second feature is the repression of private capital mobility. Faced with the flight of wealth toward more favorable jurisdictions, states react not with concessions but with restrictions: capital controls, tax disincentives for expatriation, invasive anti-avoidance rules, physical-presence requirements for large firms operating domestically. This is not only about recovering revenue: it is about reasserting lost power. In this scenario, the rule becomes clear: if you want to benefit from our market, you must abide by our conditions. Capital loses the freedom to treat the state like an airport; it must once again recognize it as an authority.

The third element is the political revalorization of the national middle class, the traditional source of democratic legitimacy. To justify their new assertiveness, states must rebuild an internal pact: protecting jobs, supporting domestic production, preventing offshoring, investing in public infrastructure. It is a selective return to welfare—not for equity, but for stability. Hard economic nationalism cannot rest on coercion alone: it needs consent. And consent is built by promising economic security, even at the cost of sacrificing some global efficiency.

The fourth feature is the direct confrontation with global private elites. In this scenario, elites are no longer partners in governance: they become objects of discipline. States may impose genuine— not symbolic— wealth taxes; seize extraordinary profits; limit the concentration of power in digital platforms; establish public infrastructure in sectors currently dominated by private actors. It is a world in which the rhetoric of "tax the rich" stops being a moralizing gesture and becomes a punitive one. No longer "pay your fair share," but "pay because we have allowed you too much power."

The fifth element is internal geopolitical polarization. In many countries, the reaction of global elites would be fierce: strategic relocations, brain drain, international lawsuits, media campaigns.

Hard economic nationalism produces not only conflict between states, but conflict within states—between a political power seeking to reclaim lost ground and an economic power unwilling to relinquish it. Societies are dangerously split between those who want protection and those who want to remain in the global system.

The sixth and perhaps most unsettling feature is the emergence of a new form of democratic authoritarianism: formally pluralistic, but substantively centralized. Because when a state decides to discipline mobile capital, it must inevitably discipline internal dissent as well. The logic is always the same: one cannot protect economic sovereignty without controlling communication, digital infrastructure, and social movements that could align with external powers. Democracy survives, but becomes conditioned by the overarching goal of national stability.

In the end, the long-term outcome hinges on one crucial question: can the state truly reclaim what it has lost? Or is the world now too interdependent for a full return to sovereignty to be sustainable? Hard economic nationalism could generate a brief moment of strength followed by a long period of stagnation; or it could produce an unexpected global rebalancing, leading to new, more stable forms of multipolar order.

This scenario is neither desirable nor inevitable. But it is possible. And the mere fact that it is considered possible is already a signal: when a society sees the return of economic nationalism as realistic, it means it has stopped believing in the global system's ability to produce legitimacy. Globalization does not die from ideological opposition; it dies when it no longer convinces. In that vacuum, the state attempts to return. But those who return are not always the same as those who left.

Why the Middle Class Is Disappearing

THE REAL IMPACT OF REFORMS

When people talk about "reforms"—whether tax, labor, welfare, education, or healthcare reforms—the public discourse tends to present them as neutral, technical instruments designed to make the system more efficient or more equitable. But their real impact over the last thirty years has been neither neutral nor technical: it has been selective. Reforms have favored two poles—the global elite and the most vulnerable groups—while progressively eroding the economic, cultural, and symbolic space of the middle class. Even the reforms that claim to protect it often end up harming it, because the middle class is the only group stable enough to bear the cost of transformations and weak enough to be unable to avoid them. Thus a fundamental part of contemporary society—the part that once ensured democratic stability, social mobility, and trust in institutions—is thinning out to the point of near disappearance.

The first effect of reforms concerns real, not nominal, taxation. Direct taxes on middle incomes have risen or remained high, while the fiscal pressure on mobile capital has decreased or shifted toward extraterritorial agreements that are nearly impossible to capture. The middle class, lacking both tax-optimization strategies and the ability to relocate, pays the full burden of a system that paradoxically claims to target the rich. Reforms that "promise fairness" therefore end up weighing on the only group that cannot escape them. The rhetoric of "tax the rich" here resembles a drape covering a different structure: not redistribution downward, but redistribution of the burden toward the center.

The second effect is tied to the transformation of the labor market. Reforms inspired by flexibility and global competitiveness have progressively weakened what once guaranteed the middle class existential stability: long-term contracts, predictable careers, wages tied to productivity, rights accompanying working life. Work has become variable, intermittent, fragmented, often deprived of the protective mechanisms that allowed people to plan for the future. The middle class has lost not only income, but horizon: the ability to imagine a coherent path, improvement, a legacy to pass on. Social mobility—once the promise and condition of modernity—has become rare, almost mythical.

The third impact concerns the exponential rise in essential costs: housing, education, healthcare, energy. These costs do not rise linearly; they rise as if responding to global logics independent of national wages. Housing becomes a financial asset driven by investors, not a consumption good; higher education becomes an entry gate to the global market, with costs reflecting international competition; healthcare depends on technologies and pharmaceuticals produced by global oligopolies; energy is tied to complex geopolitical dynamics. The middle class is squeezed in between: the poor receive subsidies; the rich absorb the costs. Those in the middle carry everything without receiving protection.

The fourth impact comes from automation and the technocratization of work, which hit intermediate professions hardest: administrative workers, skilled technicians, consultants, non-hyper-specialized professionals. Reforms that incentivize technological innovation often fail to accompany these shifts with credible reskilling policies. The result is a polarized market: highly paid jobs for a few hyper-specialists, essential but underpaid jobs for everyone else. It is the collapse of the central rung of the social ladder.

The fifth and perhaps most invisible impact concerns the redistribution of risk. Economic risk, once absorbed by the state through public policies, is increasingly transferred onto individuals: contributory pension systems, private insurance, healthcare funds, job precarity, personal responsibility for managing systemic crises. The middle class is neither poor enough to be protected nor rich enough to protect itself. It becomes an exposed, vulnerable, isolated category, yet still responsible for its own fate. It is a cruel paradox: the group that sustains the system the most receives the least in return.

Finally, the sixth impact concerns the cultural dimension of the middle class: its symbolic identity. The dominant narrative of the last decades—the narrative of competitive meritocracy, global mobility, individual creativity—has eroded the collective dignity of the middle class, portraying it as a residue of the industrial past. Reforms that celebrate innovation only deepen this perception: what is stable is obsolete; what is rooted is backward; what is predictable is inefficient. The middle class stops being the heart of the nation and becomes a segment to be upgraded, a problem to be solved. Its disappearance is thus not only economic: it is cultural, psychological, narrative.

In this scenario, global elites prosper, vulnerable groups are protected just enough to avoid social unrest, and the middle class—the historical subject of liberal democracy—shrinks until it becomes a symbolic minority. Reforms, far from being neutral instruments of progress, appear for what they really are: devices that redistribute not only income, but the very possibility of mattering. And when the middle class ceases to matter, democracy ceases to breathe.

WHY REDISTRIBUTION IS A FICTION

For decades, the word *redistribution* has held a privileged place in political vocabulary, as if it named a concrete mechanism capable of correcting inequality, rebalancing opportunity, and restoring to the middle and working classes what the economic structure takes away. But in contemporary practice, redistribution has become a functional fiction: a ritual promise masking opposite dynamics, a language that reassures without truly transforming, an idea that survives because it protects the legitimacy of the system rather than altering it. Redistribution does not happen because the system does not want it—and it does not want it because real redistribution would amount to a direct attack on the mechanisms that keep the system alive.

The first reason redistribution is a fiction lies in the global nature of capital. Mobile wealth can shift from one jurisdiction to another instantly, evading taxes, regulations, and oversight. Nation-states, by contrast, remain territorial structures—slow, bounded, and unable to move. Effective redistribution would require the ability to tax wealth coherently wherever it resides; but that ability does not exist. Any attempt to increase tax progressivity risks producing the opposite result: accelerating capital flight toward more favorable environments. To avoid hemorrhage, states end up taxing not mobile capital but immobile capital: wages, domestic savings, and the property of the middle class. The promised redistribution becomes, in practice, a redistribution in reverse.

The second reason is that redistribution collides with the fiscal fragility of modern states. Advanced economies must sustain extremely costly healthcare, pension, education, and welfare systems. Public spending grows faster than real economic output; debt rises; tax reforms are designed not to redistribute but to plug structural holes. In this context, every discussion of redistribution becomes a discussion about budget sustainability, not justice. Taxation does not correct inequality; it keeps the system from collapsing. Redistribution is proclaimed as an ethical principle but deployed as an accounting tool—moral language on the surface, fiscal necessity underneath.

The third reason is the growing privatization of essential infrastructures. When education, healthcare, transport, energy, communication, and data are—directly or indirectly—in private hands, redistribution becomes ineffective: the state transfers resources to citizens only for them to spend those resources on services controlled by profit-driven actors. Redistribution turns into an indirect subsidy to the private system. The state distributes income; the market absorbs it. The citizen receives a benefit, but the real cost of basic services rises faster than the transfer. It is a closed loop: superficially progressive, structurally regressive.

The fourth reason is cultural and political. Redistribution presupposes a society capable of conceiving justice as the reduction of inequality, whereas the contemporary paradigm conceives justice as equal access to the starting line, not as a rebalancing of the finish line. Meritocracy—understood ideologically—turns every economic difference into a difference in worth: those who have more "deserve" more. Redistribution threatens this narrative and is tolerated only when symbolic, never structural. The system therefore favors policies that do not change the architecture of opportunity: vouchers, targeted rebates, temporary bonuses—small transfers that soothe without altering the social hierarchy. This is cosmetic redistribution, not structural surgery.

The fifth reason lies in the communicative power of global elites. They know that serious redistribution would increase the authority of the state and diminish their own. Therefore they skillfully endorse a rhetoric of justice that never becomes action. They promote symbolic taxes, moral appeals, and philanthropic initiatives that fill the narrative void without filling the real one. Philanthropy in particular functions as privatized redistribution: it allows elites to decide when, how much, and to whom to give, while preserving their power to define what counts as "good." It is a form of redistribution that redistributes no power—indeed, it consolidates it.

Finally, redistribution is a fiction because contemporary inequality is not merely economic—it is structural. It is embedded in the mechanisms of financialization, digitalization, global platforms, polarized labor markets, intellectual property regimes, and technological concentration. No tax can correct what is produced by architectures of power operating beyond the reach of states. Redistribution attempts to rebalance effects without touching causes. It is like pouring water into a bucket full of holes: it creates the illusion of filling, but the level never rises.

For this reason, in many advanced democracies redistribution is no longer a practice—it is a myth. A useful, reassuring, politically marketable myth, but one lacking the transformative capacity attributed to it. It is not the product of deliberate deception; it is the outcome of a system that has internalized its own inability to correct inequality without undermining the pillars that sustain it. And so redistribution survives as language rather than reality: a way for the system to say it *wants* to be just, even when it can no longer afford to be.

The Movement in the Western World

WHO THE PROMOTERS ARE, THEIR STRATEGIES, AND HOW THE RHETORIC SHIFTS FROM COUNTRY TO COUNTRY

ITALY

In Italy, the "tax the rich" movement has established itself as a discourse, not as a project. It is an eminently rhetorical phenomenon—capable of producing slogans, media campaigns, and moral indignation, yet structurally incapable of turning into a coherent program. This is not due to a lack of political will, but to the very nature of the Italian system: a country where the tax structure is already highly progressive on labor, extremely weak on mobile capital, ineffective in combating systemic tax evasion, and chronically dependent on the middle class as the State's financial backbone. In this context, talking about "taxing the rich" becomes an exercise in political staging: a way of displaying courage without actually having to practice it.

The main promoters of this rhetoric fall into three categories—rarely in dialogue with one another, yet converging on the same language:

the parliamentary left, the media-savvy academic world, and the new progressive urban elite.

The Italian left—from the Democratic Party and its satellites to figures such as Elly Schlein and the intellectual remnants of the former radical left—uses the slogan to recover a lost social legitimacy. "Tax the rich" becomes an identity marker, useful for distinguishing themselves from the right at a time when economic, social, and even cultural issues often collapse into unexpected convergences. But the left knows it cannot move beyond rhetoric: any substantive reform would shift the fiscal burden from employees to capital, thereby upsetting the fragile alliance with the urban professional classes—the true holders of progressive consensus. This is why their proposals always remain superficial: symbolic micro-wealth taxes, inheritance taxes "only on very high thresholds," extraordinary levies never quantified. It is a ritual of self-affirmation, not a redistribution strategy.

The second category consists of economists and analysts who find in the idea of fiscal justice an ideal platform for building public visibility. Some act in good faith, driven by genuine concern for inequality; others use the narrative to brand themselves as "courageous experts" without confronting the real issue: that any increase in the pressure on large capital requires a state capacity for enforcement that Italy simply does not possess. Thus the academic discourse drifts into abstraction:

theoretical models, counterfactual calculations, calls for "seriousness" that never touch the structural point. A poor state cannot be fixed by taxing those who can relocate anywhere; it can be fixed only by reforming the state itself—but no one says this.

The third category—perhaps the most interesting—is the new progressive urban elite: managers, digital professionals, creatives, consultants, tech and cultural entrepreneurs. These are not the very rich, but the "almost rich," who adopt the rhetoric as a form of moral distinction. Using the expression "tax the rich" allows them to assume an ethical profile without putting their material position at risk. It is a kind of symbolic cleansing, a low-cost morality: they proclaim the need to tax the rich knowing that any real reform would not affect them—neither their modest assets nor their incomes, still too low to fall into the highest tax brackets. Those who truly hold wealth in Italy do not speak, do not promote, do not expose themselves: they have no need to.

As for the State, it embraces this rhetoric as a surrogate for moral authority. Talking about justice helps cover the inability to enforce it. The Italian system cannot genuinely monitor wealth, cannot accurately map financial assets, cannot sustainably confront multinational corporations. This is why the debate shifts to symbolism: the "rich" are discussed as an abstract category, not as a concrete set of legally identifiable subjects. It is a discourse that consoles the public without committing power to action.

Thus the strategy in Italy takes on a typically Mediterranean form: moral mobilization without consequences. Proposals circulate in talk shows, editorials, virtual squares, even official speeches; but they melt away like snow in the sun as soon as they meet parliamentary reality. No party is willing to shoulder the structural transformations that the idea would require: land registry reform, systemic VAT-evasion enforcement, revision of property taxation, integration of databases, abolition of micro-preferential regimes, creation of a real wealth-tax system. All these measures require an administrative sovereignty Italy has lost—and which no one dares to rebuild.

Finally, there is something deeply Italian in all this: the rhetoric of "taxing the rich" never targets the real rich, but the imaginary rich. The target is always someone unknown: the heiress, the rentier, the great evader, the faceless billionaire. Never the local professional with a second apartment, never the small-town entrepreneur, never the political class, never the para-state sector. The rich are always someone else. This makes the slogan perfect: morally impeccable, technically harmless, politically profitable.

In Italy, therefore, the "tax the rich" movement is a theater. Not in the pejorative sense, but in the anthropological one: a collective performance that allows society to imagine itself as just while remaining unjust, and allows the State to imagine itself strong while remaining weak. This is why the rhetoric thrives: because it does not require anyone to actually do what they say.

And because, like all well-crafted fictions, it is more comforting than the truth.

FRANCE

In France, the rhetoric of "taxing the rich" occupies an ambiguous—almost schizophrenic—position, because here more than anywhere else fiscal justice is an integral part of national identity. The Republic was born from the idea that private wealth must constantly be brought back within the perimeter of the collective; and yet contemporary France is one of the Western countries where the real pressure on great wealth is more fragile, more easily circumvented, and more symbolic than tradition would suggest. The result is a country that *speaks* like an egalitarian democracy but *acts* like a system deeply afraid of touching its true holders of capital, for fear of accelerating their flight. The rhetoric remains revolutionary; the practice, increasingly cautious.

In this context, the "tax the rich" movement is fueled by a constellation of actors who rarely share a common vision but converge on the same language because that language performs an essential function: preserving the *imaginary* of justice in a country that can no longer produce justice in practice. The post-socialist left—reduced to a sentimental minority with little influence over what remains of the popular electorate—continues to invoke a wealth tax as an identity symbol, more an act of memory than of governance. *La France Insoumise* turns the slogan into a banner of conflict, but its discursive strength runs up against a structural limit: a movement composed of precarious youth, urban employees, and disillusioned working classes can mobilize the streets, but it cannot run the fiscal machinery of a complex nation. And then there is Macron's centrist bloc, whose relationship with wealth has been ambivalent from the beginning: abolishing the wealth tax on the one hand, and invoking "fiscal solidarity" on the other. Macron eliminated what France considered its redistributive symbol—and paid a very high political price for it. Since then, any reference he makes to fiscal justice is calibrated to avoid another social earthquake like the *Gilets Jaunes*, which erupted not as a revolt against the rich, but as a revolt against a State perceived as the defender of the rich.

France's apparent strength in fiscal matters—its centralized system, its competent administration, its egalitarian tradition—thus flips into its opposite. The great state machine is extremely powerful when targeting those who are visible, rooted, and sedentary; but it becomes fragile when facing mobile wealth, financial assets, digital holdings, and large entrepreneurial families who can relocate to Brussels, London, or Geneva within months. France remains one of the most heavily taxed countries in Europe, but the burden falls almost entirely on wage earners, pensioners, and the middle class—those who cannot move. This is why the rhetoric of *taxer les riches* has an eminently symbolic function: it keeps alive the idea of a just Republic while reality shifts toward an ever sharper polarization.

Within this scenario, the promoters of the rhetoric are not acting to implement a real wealth tax: they are managing an imaginary. The left uses it for self-identification; the center to reassure; activists to protest; economists to keep alive a debate that, in practice, lacks instruments. The State, for its part, knows perfectly well that a truly incisive intervention would risk eroding what remains of the tax base and destabilizing social equilibrium. France has already been the stage of the largest fiscal insurrection in Europe this century; no one wishes to repeat the experience. Thus, taxing the rich becomes a ritual formula: spoken emphatically, yet suspended in a limbo where no one has an interest in making it real.

In France, more than elsewhere, the rhetoric of "taxing the rich" is a way of saving the country's collective identity. It is a language that allows the French to imagine themselves egalitarian while the real structure drifts away from equality. It is a fiction the State uses to protect itself from the revolution it both evokes and fears. And it is this tension between myth and reality that makes the French case so emblematic: a nation that preserves justice as its founding ideal, yet practices only its shadow. A country that speaks as if political power still controlled the system, while mobile capital has already shifted its center of gravity elsewhere. A country that invokes justice not to achieve it, but to prevent its absence from igniting a new social fire.

GERMANY

In Germany, the rhetoric of "taxing the rich" has never taken on the emotional tone found in France or Italy: here taxation is neither an identity banner nor a political weapon, but an area governed by an institutional culture that privileges balance, gradualism, and administrative prudence. And yet, in recent years, this rhetoric has begun to circulate with growing insistence in Germany as well—not driven by redistributive passions, but by the perception that the German economic model, built for decades on exports, cheap energy, and demographic stability, has entered a phase of structural decline. When a system once considered solid begins to crack, the need to identify "who must pay" becomes inevitable; and so Germany finds itself debating fiscal justice not out of ideological inclination, but out of systemic necessity.

Here, the promoters of the "tax the rich" movement belong to a political ecosystem very different from that of other European countries. The Greens and the SPD—its main drivers—are not radical or anti-system forces; they are governing parties, integrated into the very core of state machinery. This gives their discourse a character that is at once moderate and insistent: it does not promise revolutions but adjustments; it does not denounce the wealthy as an enemy class, but asks them for a "responsible contribution." The key word in Germany is not justice but *Verantwortung*—responsibility. Taxing the rich is presented not as a punitive act, but as one of the ways in which German society might finance the energy transition, digitalization, defense, and the modernization of increasingly obsolete infrastructure.

And yet this rhetoric collides with a structural limit: Germany remains one of the few European countries with a large, rooted, fiscally disciplined, and politically influential middle class. It is a *productive* middle class, not a consumerist one—made up of small and medium enterprises, specialized professionals, and an industrial stratum that forms the backbone of the economic system. Any discourse on "taxing the rich" runs up against this reality: in Germany it is far harder to identify a distant, hyper-mobile elite like those in France or the United States. German wealth is diffuse, not concentrated; embedded in the productive fabric; distributed through a system of ownership that rewards stability rather than rent. Those who speak of "the rich" in Germany often, unintentionally, mean the *Mittelstand*—and no governing party can afford to alienate this social bloc.

This is why the debate remains suspended in an ambiguous zone. On one side, the SPD and the Greens continue to propose the return of a wealth tax, especially to finance public investments that no government can cover through the ordinary budget. On the other side, the CDU/CSU oppose it firmly, invoking the risk of harming the competitiveness of family-owned industrial firms —and, unlike in other countries, this opposition does not appear as a defense of "the rich" but as a defense of national economic identity. Even many progressive voters fear that a real wealth tax would hit local entrepreneurs more than global capital.

Within this unstable balance emerges the true nature of redistributive rhetoric in Germany: it is not a leftward push, but an attempt to reconcile a very expensive social model with a tax base that no longer suffices. The country needs money—for the energy transition, AI, the military, demographics—but does not want to admit that its fiscal system is no longer adequate to sustain this new historical phase. Speaking of "taxing the rich" thus becomes a way of postponing the real question: not who must pay, but how much longer Germany can continue paying to preserve its model of prosperity.

This rhetoric also reveals a deeper phenomenon: the growing gap between Germany's economic self-image and its contemporary reality. The country still perceives itself as a stable, efficient, cohesive industrial power; but in practice it is fractured by territorial divides, loss of competitiveness, demographic decline, and a rapid erosion of its industrial advantage. At such a moment, invoking "tax the rich" helps safeguard the idea that Germany can face the future without questioning its foundations. It is a reassuring narrative: ask a bit more from the affluent, and the model will continue. But it is a narrative that evades the harsher conflict: Germany is no longer Europe's stable scaffolding, and its social model is no longer automatically financeable.

The German case is thus almost the negative image of the French. In France the rhetoric is incendiary because the State is strong in form and weak in substance; in Germany it is moderate because the State is still relatively solid, yet fears it may not remain so. In France the slogan serves to pacify; in Germany, to avoid acknowledging decline. In both cases, however, "taxing the rich" is not a project but a symbolic defense of an order that no longer knows how to sustain itself. Germany, with its fiscal discipline and culture of responsibility, appears the country least suited to a radical redistributive discourse—and precisely for that reason it is where the language of fiscal justice becomes most transparent: a language that does not aim to change reality, but to delay the moment when reality must be confronted.

SPAIN

In Spain, the rhetoric of "taxing the rich" does not arise—as it does in other countries—from a need to rebuild state legitimacy or from a collapse of social mobility, but from something more specific and more combustible: the country's internal fracture. Here, the fiscal question is not simply a confrontation between rich and poor, but a conflict between territories, identities, and competing social models. Spain is the place where "tax the rich" immediately becomes *tax Madrid*, *tax Catalonia*, *tax the privileges of the wealthy regions*, and where redistribution overlaps with a deeper, unresolved national debate about the relationship between the central state and its autonomous communities. Fiscal discourse is therefore the visible surface of a political tension that has never stopped simmering beneath the skin of the State.

The chief promoter of this rhetoric in recent years has been the Spanish left, especially in its more radical branch: Podemos, later Sumar, and the intellectual ecosystem surrounding them. These movements have turned the taxation of the rich into a moral and identity-based banner—a way to oppose finance, large corporations, real-estate funds, and to differentiate themselves from traditional social democracy, perceived as too compromised with market logics. Yet unlike other European lefts, Podemos succeeded in anchoring its rhetoric in real, measurable, deeply rooted distress: the devastating impact of the 2008 crisis,

Europe's highest youth unemployment rate, chronic precarity, and the near impossibility for young people to enter the housing market. In Spain, talking about fiscal justice is not an intellectual gesture: it is an immediate response to a still-open collective wound.

What makes the Spanish case particularly complex, however, is the role of the Comunidad de Madrid, which over the last twenty years has developed a fiscal strategy diametrically opposed to that of the central left: lower taxes, abolition of the wealth tax, incentives for investment, and an aggressive management of internal tax competition. Madrid has transformed itself into a kind of domestic free port, attracting entrepreneurs, investors, and high-income professionals from across the country. Its economic and demographic growth, fueled by this policy, has polarized the debate: for the left, it is the symbol of a "paradise for the rich"; for the right, it is the victorious model of competitiveness and economic freedom. The "tax the rich" rhetoric in Spain thus became immediately intertwined with the perception of an imbalanced quasi-federal system in which some regions feel penalized by central fiscal redistribution, while others are accused of draining the tax base from the rest of the country.

Prime Minister Sánchez has navigated these forces with considerable political skill, using redistributive rhetoric as a glue for an otherwise fragile and territorially heterogeneous coalition. The proposal to introduce a temporary wealth tax on large fortunes was the perfect example of this ambiguity: a measure announced with moralizing tone, designed to project progressive courage, yet calibrated so as not to truly affect mobile or internationalized wealth. It was more of a political statement than a reform—effective for shaping an image, but insufficient to transform the structure of inequality.

Spain, like Australia and Canada, is also a country in which inequality in the housing market plays a decisive role. Major cities—Madrid, Barcelona, Valencia—have become magnets for global investors, real-estate funds, and tourist platforms such as Airbnb, pushing the cost of living to levels unreachable for much of the population. The "tax the rich" rhetoric thus grafts itself onto a real sense of malaise, driven not primarily by ultra-wealthy individuals but by the perception that the housing market is dominated by actors foreign to the local community. Yet, as in Australia, intervening seriously in this system would mean challenging a massive share of national capital, as well as a sector that sustains a crucial portion of GDP. And so, even in Spain, rhetoric stops at the threshold of reality.

Finally, the most destabilizing factor of all is territorial nationalism. In Catalonia, the Basque Country, and other regions with strong local identities, fiscal discourse is directly linked to the question of self-determination. For many independence supporters, "tax the rich" effectively means "tax Madrid" —a way of freeing themselves from a system they perceive as unjust. For others, it means preventing wealthy regions from retaining too much of their own revenue. In this context, rhetoric does not define a relationship between individuals and the State, but between territories that see themselves in competition for survival.

The Spanish case thus reveals a unique trait in the Western landscape: here, "tax the rich" is not merely a redistributive fiction—it is a political hotspot, a language through which long-standing social and territorial tensions find expression when no other form seems adequate. It is the symptom of a country attempting to preserve minimal cohesion as its internal balances continuously shift. A rhetoric that says far less about the rich than about Spain's difficulty in recognizing—and governing—its own fragmentation.

UNITED KINGDOM

In the United Kingdom, the "tax the rich" movement takes a form radically different from its continental counterparts. It does not arise from the French republican tradition, nor from Italy's Catholic-social morality, nor from Germany's redistributive prudence: it arises from a collapse of trust. Since 2008, British society has progressively internalized the idea that the system is rigged, that there exists a financial and property-owning elite immune to the ordinary rule of law, and that politics is hostage to donors, lobby groups, and private think tanks. In the UK, taxing the rich is therefore not an ideological banner: it is a gesture of repair—a way to re-establish a minimum bond between citizens and institutions after decades of privatization, disinvestment, and economic polarization.

The main promoter of this rhetoric is the post-Corbyn progressive left, which has had to reinvent itself after the trauma of 2019. If Corbyn infused the word "redistribution" with near-moral fervor, the new Labour Party uses it as an instrument of normalization: it seeks to appear responsible, competent, business-friendly but not submissive, capable of raising revenue without frightening the markets. "Tax the rich" thus becomes a calibrated, almost accounting-like formula: not a revolutionary manifesto but a proposal presented as necessary to fill holes left by years of austerity. In the UK—unlike in Italy or France—the left does not use fiscal rhetoric to define itself; it uses it to prove its reliability. Fiscal justice is deployed to reassure working-class and middle-class voters without overly alarming the City.

At the same time, the UK is also the Western country where the economic-financial elite is most powerful, sophisticated, and agile. London is the global heart of fiscal and corporate arbitrage: an ecosystem in which trusts, special-purpose vehicles, special residency regimes, offshore structures, and legal protections form an impenetrable barrier. In the UK, taxing the rich almost always means taxing those who lack the means to avoid taxation: well-paid professionals, local property owners, skilled workers, small businesses. The truly wealthy—the ones the slogan is ostensibly aimed at—are often out of reach. And the political system knows this perfectly well.

This dynamic produces a specific form of hypocrisy: the UK is perhaps the country where people talk the most about taxing wealth, and yet where it is most difficult to do so. The City is not only an economic center: it is an informal political power, capable of issuing vetoes, influencing governments, and threatening capital flight with a credibility few global actors possess. It is telling that whenever a British government has attempted to introduce more incisive measures—the disastrous "mini-budget crisis" of 2022 being the clearest example—the market's reaction has been immediate, brutal, and destabilizing enough to topple a prime minister within weeks. In this context, "tax the rich" is a protected language: one may invoke it, but only within limits compatible with the financial order.

Another peculiarity is the weight of real estate, which in Britain is the true infrastructure of wealth. London and the South-East have become magnets for global capital—often opaque—transforming housing into a financial asset detached from local incomes. For millions of Britons, taxing the rich would paradoxically mean taxing themselves: the urban middle class whose homes have been inflated far beyond their real purchasing power. This ambiguity prevents an honest conversation and produces an abstract discourse always aimed at some undefined "other": foreign oligarchs, hedge funds, large global landlords. Never at the neighbour in Islington or Kensington.

Finally, the UK is undergoing a profound identity crisis after Brexit. Leaving the EU did not restore sovereignty; it revealed how fragile the country's economic fabric truly was. The welfare state is exhausted, the health system is collapsing, wages stagnate, social mobility evaporates. In this situation, "tax the rich" becomes a narrative shortcut: the simple answer to a set of problems that no longer have simple solutions. It is the way the nation tries to preserve its idea of justice while reality crumbles beneath it.

The UK thus exemplifies how a slogan can circulate through society without ever finding a concrete landing point. For the left, it is a soft identity code; for moderates, a way to gain support without alarming the markets; for citizens, a cry of frustration against an elite seen as unreachable; for the markets, mere background noise. It is a discourse that serves everyone and changes nothing. And that is precisely why it thrives: because there is no country where the distance between real wealth and the State's capacity to discipline it is greater, more visible, and more immovable.

UNITED STATES

In the United States, the "tax the rich" movement is—more than anywhere else—a cultural battle before it is a political one. This is where the slogan was born, where it radicalized, where it found charismatic interpreters and implacable opponents, and where it embodies a clash between two opposing visions of society: on one side, meritocratic, property-owning America, convinced that wealth is proof of virtue; on the other, a disillusioned, impoverished America which—after forty years of wage stagnation and the vertiginous rise of the techno-financial elite—no longer believes in the myth of social mobility. In no other Western country does the idea of taxing the rich carry such anthropological weight: it is not about fiscal policy; it is about the very meaning of individual fate.

The protagonists of the rhetoric are unmistakable: Bernie Sanders, Elizabeth Warren, Alexandria Ocasio-Cortez, the left wing of the Democratic Party, and increasingly, a wide section of progressive American culture—from academic think tanks to media platforms. Yet the essential point is that in America, "taxing the rich" is not a technical concept: it is a symbol of rupture with the neoliberal order, a way of declaring that American capitalism no longer works as a collective promise. Sanders and Warren have turned taxation into a moral referendum on the wealthiest 1%; AOC has transformed it into a generational, almost existential battle. For millions of young Americans, growing up means discovering that working is not enough, studying is not enough, innovating is not enough: the very structure of the system is oriented toward concentrating wealth in a handful of decision-making nodes—almost always digital, almost always Californian, almost always unreachable. "Tax the rich" thus becomes the phrase that encapsulates an entire generation's disillusionment.

Yet the United States is also the country where extreme wealth has built one of the world's most impenetrable systems of legal and political protection. America is where great wealth engages in lobbying, finances electoral campaigns, controls digital infrastructures, influences think tanks, and shapes public opinion with a power unknown elsewhere. American corporations are not merely businesses: they are geopolitical actors, with budgets larger than those of nation-states, enormous deterrent capacity, and total global mobility. In this sense, "taxing the rich" in the United States means confronting an economic power that is constitutional—not external to the State, but incorporated into its functioning. Congress itself is permeated by interests directly or indirectly financed by economic elites.

The result is a tension with no outlet: on one hand, a vast portion of the population demands fiscal justice; on the other, the institutions are so intertwined with great wealth that any meaningful intervention becomes nearly impossible. Every progressive proposal ends up crushed between three forces: the Supreme Court, which defends the principle of economic freedom; the Senate, which represents conservative states with deeply anti-tax political cultures; and the campaign-finance system, which makes every election dependent on large donors.

There is, however, a new element: Silicon Valley. In recent years, a significant segment of the American tech elite has begun using "tax the rich" rhetoric as a tool of moral legitimization. This is not self-critique; it is strategy. Certain progressive-leaning entrepreneurs—especially from the digital world, not traditional finance—have understood that publicly supporting higher taxes on great fortunes strengthens their image as "builders of the future," shields them from accusations of media monopoly, and positions them as ethically acceptable interlocutors for the progressive left. It is the American version of what you described in earlier chapters: philanthropy as soft power, morality as shield, taxation as insurance against delegitimization.

There is another peculiarly American dimension: the religious undertone of the discourse. In the United States, money is a sign of individual accomplishment—almost a blessing. For this reason, taxing the rich is perceived by many as an injustice against those who "worked hard." America is the country where the entrepreneur is a hero and failure a moral flaw. Progressive rhetoric, with its call for structural redistribution, touches nerves that destabilize not only the economic order but the national imaginary itself. The conflict is not political; it is mythical.

All this makes the American case the most emblematic of all—not because the rich are richer, not because inequality is greater, but because in the United States "tax the rich" stands at the center of a struggle for the country's soul. For some, it is the condition for saving democracy; for others, it is a sign of socialist drift; for others still, a progressive charade that will never materialize. The truth, as always, lies elsewhere: the discourse thrives because it cannot be realized. It is a language that expresses a real fracture but cannot be translated into law without threatening the entire constitutional and economic architecture of the United States.

In America, more than anywhere else, taxing the rich is a battle that defines collective identity, not fiscal policy. It is the symptom of a nation unsure whether to believe in its founding myth or declare it broken. It is the slogan that says everything and changes nothing—because everything that would have to change is precisely what the system cannot afford to touch.

CANADA

In Canada, the "tax the rich" rhetoric takes on a surprisingly distinctive character: here it does not arise as a radical gesture or as a response to social collapse, but as an organic part of the country's progressive self-image. Canada likes to see itself as morally balanced, moderate, civil—a nation in which fiscal justice has increasingly become a kind of certificate of political good conduct. Yet it is precisely this apparent normality that hides the most interesting feature of the Canadian case: the rhetoric is so deeply integrated into public discourse that it has become a sort of reflex, a slogan that resurfaces cyclically without ever producing the structural transformation it promises. Canada is the perfect laboratory for understanding how a system can use redistributive rhetoric not to correct inequality, but to manage it.

The discourse is fueled primarily by Justin Trudeau's Liberals, who over the past decade have built an important part of their political identity around presenting themselves as the responsible, progressive version of North America. For Trudeau, talking about taxing the rich is not a revolutionary act but a way of differentiating Canada from the United States, of crafting an image of fiscal civility that appeals to the urban, educated, multicultural electorate of major cities. It is a perfect language for modern Canada: reassuring, polished, seemingly pragmatic. But in practice, the real tax pressure on great wealth has not risen significantly, while the middle class—like everywhere else—remains the financial backbone of the system.

On the other side are the New Democrats (NDP), who represent the most sincere and structurally coherent version of "tax the rich" rhetoric in the Canadian landscape. Their discourse is more radical, more explicit, more internally consistent: wealth taxes, levies on large real-estate holdings, higher corporate taxation, steep inheritance contributions. But the NDP does not govern; and when it props up a Liberal government, it does so without enough leverage to impose its priorities. Thus the rhetoric remains programmatic rather than governmental: a promise that defines the party more than a policy that defines the country.

The third actor shaping the discourse is Canada's academic and media culture—one of the most progressive and influential in the Western hemisphere. From universities to public broadcasters, Canada produces a constant stream of reports, editorials, studies, and campaigns advocating for fairer taxation of wealth. It is a culture that deeply believes in the role of the state and sees redistribution as a natural component of collective ethics. But it is also a culture that lives with a structural paradox: mobile wealth flees Canada just as easily as it flees any other jurisdiction. The analytical power is there; the coercive power is not.

Canada's peculiarity also emerges in the centrality of real estate. In cities like Toronto and Vancouver, wealth is concentrated almost pathologically in housing assets whose values have surged far beyond local incomes over the past twenty years. In this context, talking about taxing the rich becomes immediately ambiguous: who are "the rich"? Global speculators? Real-estate funds? Chinese and American investors? Or the urban middle-class families who now own homes worth millions despite having ordinary salaries? This ambiguity paralyzes the discourse: every proposal risks hitting precisely those who constitute the electoral base of Canadian progressivism.

Further complicating the landscape is Canada's federal structure. Any significant tax on wealth would require coordination between Ottawa and the provinces, yet the provinces have no interest in giving up their fiscal autonomy. The result is fragmentation that prevents any truly consequential intervention: each province fears losing taxpayers to its neighbor, each local government fears appearing anti-business, each attempt at coordination runs up against a federalism that fiercely protects its fiscal perimeters. Thus, paradoxically, the very state that most believes in fiscal justice is one of the least capable of implementing it coherently.

The "tax the rich" movement in Canada is therefore a hybrid product: morally strong, politically weak, culturally dominant, fiscally ineffective. The rhetoric holds together a progressive identity that reassures the urban population, gives the academic world a common language, allows Liberals to position themselves ethically without overly alienating investors, and enables the NDP to maintain a recognizable ideological profile. But it does not alter the structure of inequality, which in Canada continues to deepen steadily—driven especially by the financialization of real estate and the stagnation of median wages.

Canada is not a country that uses "tax the rich" to mask a conflict that does not exist; it is a country that uses it to sustain its self-image as a just society while its reality quietly drifts toward a polarization it has never known. It is the gentlest, most courteous, most institutional version of redistributive fiction: a fiction articulated without cynicism, yet with a calmness that makes its symbolic nature even more evident. A promise that comforts without changing; a language that unifies without transforming; an identity that shields the nation from the anxiety of decline, but does nothing to stop it.

AUSTRALIA

In Australia, the "tax the rich" discourse takes on yet another tone, distinct from that of other Western countries: less ideological than in the United States, less identity-driven than in Canada, less dramatic than in France, less theatrical than in Italy, and less technocratic than in Germany. It is a pragmatic, almost engineering-like discourse—one that resurfaces whenever the system perceives a growing imbalance in the cost of living, in property ownership, or in personal taxation. Yet this very pragmatism reveals Australia's central paradox: for decades it was one of the most egalitarian societies in the Western world, and yet today it has become a highly advanced laboratory of economic polarization. In this context, "tax the rich" does not arise as an ideological demand but as the symptom of a quietly growing civic discomfort.

The main force driving this rhetoric is the Labor Party, especially in its post-2010 incarnation, which progressively introduced the theme of fiscal justice in response to two explosive trends: the housing-affordability crisis and the enormous growth of financial wealth relative to wages. In Australia, more than elsewhere, inequality does not show up in the manager's salary or the professional's income—its epicenter is the price of housing. Entire generations of young Australians—almost unthinkable just a few decades ago—can no longer afford to buy a home. And when housing becomes unattainable, fiscal rhetoric becomes inevitable: taxing the rich appears to be the only way to rebalance a system that has transformed an essential good into a speculative asset.

This dynamic produces an immediate consequence: the implicit target of the discourse is not global "super-rich" individuals, but large property owners, investors, pension funds that have colonized the housing market, and more broadly all those who benefit from generous property-related tax incentives (such as negative gearing and favorable capital-gains concessions). These measures, originally introduced to support the middle class, have over the years become instruments of wealth concentration. Thus, when Australians talk about "taxing the rich," they often mean "taxing property owners"—a source of intense internal tension, because in Australia property ownership is not just an economic asset but an identity marker, almost an anthropological feature. To question it is to question the country's founding narrative.

The discourse is also fueled by part of Australia's academic and civic culture, which is particularly attentive to the effects of financialization on social equality. Think tanks, economists, and public commentators emphasize the country's dangerous dependence on the housing sector, the unsustainability of private-debt levels, and the stagnation of real wages. Yet, as in Canada, analytical power does not translate into political power: many diagnoses are shared, few solutions implemented. The reason is simple: serious tax intervention risks triggering a collapse of a housing bubble that represents a vast share of national wealth. Rhetoric therefore becomes a release valve rather than a project.

Unlike many European countries, however, Australia does not have a truly radical left. Labor is neither La France Insoumise nor the party of Bernie Sanders: it is a governing party accustomed to balancing moderate reforms with middle-class protection. For this reason, its tax proposals always move within a narrow corridor: phasing out certain concessions, increasing oversight of speculative property investment, modest adjustments to top income brackets. These measures promise fairness but leave the deeper structure of Australia's inequality untouched. Meanwhile, the Liberal Party defends private property and investment incentives with an almost classically Anglo-Saxon ideological coherence, arguing that any attack on housing wealth is an attack on the nation's core.

A further structural factor is demographic: Australia has benefited enormously from skilled immigration and rapid urban growth. Urban progressive elites—particularly in Melbourne and Sydney—are partly supportive of rebalancing the system, yet many of them participate directly in the housing ecosystem that fuels inequality. Here too, rhetoric becomes a form of moral distinction: one publicly endorses fiscal justice while privately benefiting from the status quo.

The Australian case thus reveals an essential point: redistributive rhetoric tends to flourish where the system is unwilling—or unable—to touch the root of the problem. In Australia, that root is not the billionaire tech founder nor the financial corporation; it is the housing market and its central role in the formation of private wealth. Here, as elsewhere, "taxing the rich" becomes a way to avoid naming what would truly be required to rebalance society: reducing systemic dependence on housing rents, rethinking property-related tax incentives, confronting the household-debt bubble. Yet no government wants to take such a risk.

Australia therefore embodies a specific form of redistributive fiction: not the moralistic fiction of France, nor the identity-driven fiction of Italy, nor the cultural fiction of Canada, but a technical fiction—a way of making structural inequality appear manageable by framing it as a matter of tax parameters rather than of social architecture. It is a country that talks about taxing the rich as if the issue were fiscal calibration, when the real question is the model itself. And it is precisely this discrepancy between language and reality that makes the Australian case so instructive: it shows how a system can maintain its stability by endlessly discussing the cure, provided no one ever touches the disease.

Technique as the New Political Subject

Everything we have analysed so far—the new moral posture of the elites, the rhetoric of fiscal justice, the transformation of States into administrative units, the rise of private governance, the strategic use of taxation to stabilize the system—finds a striking resonance in the philosophy of Emanuele Severino.

Severino (1929–2020)—one of the most important but least internationally known European philosophers of the twentieth century—devoted his life to showing that Western civilization rests on a radical conviction: that beings come from nothing and return to nothing. From this belief—what he considered *the true madness of the West*—arises the will to bend the world, to control it, to transform it, to compensate for its fragility. And it is here, he argues, that *Technique* (with a capital "T") emerges: not as a collection of tools, but as an impersonal power seeking to increase indefinitely its capacity to modify what is.

For Severino, then, contemporary politics—even when it speaks the language of justice, redistribution, or morality—merely executes the movements dictated by Technique. What appears, on the surface, as an ethical gesture—even the elites' willingness to "have themselves taxed"—becomes an internal function of a much larger process.

Severino's "Technique" is not the ensemble of machines, algorithms, or digital infrastructures we have built. It is much more: it is the fully developed form of the ancient Western desire to dominate becoming, to force the world to obey human decision. Once the West embraced the idea that things can emerge from nothing and fall back into nothingness, it opened the door to the notion that they are available, malleable, transformable, disposable. If a being can become nothing, then everything may be treated as a means to an end.

Technique is the moment when this paradigm ceases to be a philosophical idea and becomes the actual structure of the world: the organized power that seeks to maximize, without limit, its capacity to transform. Science provides knowledge, economics calculates costs and benefits, politics coordinates and legitimizes. But the ultimate direction of movement—the unlimited increase of power—is not chosen by politics or economics: it is imposed by the logic of Technique itself. In Severino's view, Technique is the new "destiny" of the West—not capitalism, not the State, not ideology, but the necessity of expanding dominion over beings.

Seen in this light, the dynamics explored throughout this book become unmistakably connected. We have seen how contemporary elites volunteer to "be taxed," not to surrender power but to stabilize it; how States shrink into administrative operators of decisions taken elsewhere; how global governance, platforms, supranational agencies, and large investment funds become the true centres of decision. This is not simply political cunning or oligarchic conspiracy: it is the form that Technique assumes when it passes through politics.

Taxing the rich, from this perspective, is not an ethical gesture but a system parameter: a mechanism to prevent explosions, avoid instability, and maintain the minimum cohesion required for the increase of power to continue undisturbed.

Severino would say: *Technique cannot tolerate that any part of the world remain outside its control.* It must transform resistance into resource. In this sense, public anger over inequality, indignation at tax havens, resentment toward "the super-rich," are not only threats to the system—they are *information*. They reveal points of fragility, spots where power risks encountering friction. The elites' response—"tax the rich" pronounced by the rich themselves, philanthropy, symbolic fiscal reforms, support for a modest level of apparent justice—is the way Technique incorporates these resistances. It does not crush them; it *converts* them into opportunities to strengthen its legitimacy.

Thus fiscal justice becomes one of the instruments through which the system makes itself morally acceptable, and therefore more stable, and therefore more capable of pursuing its end: growth of power.

From this vantage point, elites who declare themselves ready to pay higher taxes are no longer the sovereign subjects of the game. They are functionaries of a process larger than themselves. They believe they are "doing politics," yet they are enacting what the techno-economic logic requires in order to keep expanding. Technique needs them as it needs any other device: they are its privileged interpreters, not its masters. The apparently "ethical" gesture—accepting to be taxed—becomes, in Severino's sense, a perfectly functional act within the will-to-power of Technique.

This also overturns our understanding of the State. For Severino, the modern State—born as the locus of sovereignty, ultimate command, and the monopoly of decision—gradually becomes just one function among others. It no longer determines the destiny of the world; it registers it, translates it, ratifies it. Over the long term, it is the technical powers—financial infrastructures, platforms, techno-scientific apparatuses—that determine what is possible, rational, and necessary. The State can resist for a while, but any resistance that slows the process too much generates a competitive advantage elsewhere, in another region, in another alliance between Technique and capital. It is the global competition of Technique against itself: a framework that strengthens itself precisely through conflicts between political systems.

Every State that truly attempted to "discipline wealth" would be punished by the logic of power: capital flight, isolation, decline. And so taxation of the rich can increase only within the limits compatible with the survival of the technical system—never beyond.

This explains why redistribution is, in practice, a fiction. Not because redistributive policies do not exist, but because they can operate only at the margins, never at the structural level. The structure—the concentration of power in the hands of those who control Technique—is not negotiable. It is the heart of the system. One can lighten the burden on the vulnerable, compensate the middle class, ask the very rich to contribute a little more, but one cannot make the technical power structure truly vulnerable without exposing the entire system to external competition that would overwhelm it.

In a Severinian frame, the question "Why do the rich want to be taxed?" has a precise answer: because *Technique needs their power to appear legitimate*, needs their presence to be accepted as necessary. Better to surrender a portion of income than to call into question the machine that produces that income.

At this point, a deeper question emerges: *what becomes of ethics if the true subject of history is Technique?* If the movement of the world is determined by a logic aiming at the indefinite growth of power, what room remains for responsibility, truth, or non-strategic justice?

Here we touch on the most demanding aspect of Severino's thought. His critique is not an invitation to resignation before Technique; it is the diagnosis of an original madness—the belief that things can arise from nothing and fall into nothing—from which Technique emerges as a coherent development. As long as we remain within this horizon, rebellion against Technique is merely one of its internal moments: even the fiercest moral critique is absorbed into the game, becoming feedback for better management, parameter adjustment, refinement of devices. This is what we observed in our discussion of philanthropy, corporate responsibility, symbolic taxation: ethics reduced to modulation of consent.

To escape this horizon, Severino proposes a far more radical thought, which we cannot develop here: the insight that being does not come into or go out of existence, that each thing is eternally itself, and that the nihilism of Western thought—the idea that what exists can become nothing—is the real root of our treating the world as material available for use.

But even without following Severino to his metaphysical conclusions, one core idea remains crucial for this book: the moral posture of contemporary elites—their willingness to be taxed, their offer to act as ethical guides—is not an exception within a technical world. *It is itself a technical device*.

If this is true, then the real alternative is not simply "tax more" or "tax less." It is whether we accept that the only criterion of justice is whatever increases the system's capacity to endure, govern, and transform. A justice reduced to a function of stability is no longer justice; it is maintenance.

Severino helps us see precisely this: when ethics is bent to the logic of power, it ceases to limit power and becomes its most refined mask. Technique does not present itself as domination; it presents itself as salvation. It does not say "I want everything," but "I am merely doing what is necessary." And when it speaks through the voices of elites asking to be taxed, it says essentially the same thing: "We sacrifice a little for the common good."

Thus the history of power begins again, wearing a new mask.

For this reason, the connection with Severino is not a theoretical luxury but a necessity. Without a philosophy of Technique, the behaviour of contemporary elites remains a psychological enigma or an implausible conspiracy. With Severino, that behaviour appears for what it is: the adaptation of a dominant class to a larger process that no longer needs ideologies for justification—only results.

Taxing the rich, in this horizon, is one of the ways the system *takes care of itself*.

The real question—if we still want to speak of ethics and politics in a strong sense—is whether we are willing to trade justice for maintenance, freedom for stability, responsibility for functionality. Here begins, perhaps, the book that this book is not, but that everything we have written prepares: not a book about the morality of the rich, but about the destiny of our idea of justice in the age of Technique.

Conclusion

TAXATION AS THE LANGUAGE OF POWER

Having arrived at the end of this journey, one truth emerges with clarity: the "tax the rich" movement is not a project of redistribution; it is a new device for legitimizing power. It does not arise from a genuine desire to rebalance society, but from the need of the elites to preserve their centrality in a fragmented, unstable, unpredictable world. The rhetoric of fiscal justice thus becomes a modern form of *raison d'État*—but no longer enacted by States: enacted by the elites themselves.

As we have seen, each country refracts this rhetoric through its own history and fears. In Italy, it becomes moral theatre; in France, an identity ritual meant to contain social explosion; in Germany, a way of postponing the confrontation with decline; in the United Kingdom, a symbolic gesture to rebuild trust after the dismantling of the welfare state; in the United States, a cultural battleground touching the nation's very soul; in Canada, a reflex of progressive civility; in Australia, a technical attempt to manage inequality born of the real estate system; in Spain, a language expressing unresolved territorial fractures. Each invokes justice; none touches the structure that reproduces inequality.

But the real strength of the movement lies elsewhere: in its ability to transform a potentially subversive demand—limiting the power of the elites—into a gesture that actually strengthens those very elites. Today, the wealthy do not defend themselves by denying their privilege, but by declaring it morally burdensome. They no longer exercise their power *against* the State, but *through* it. They no longer fear popular anger, because they have learned to convert it into ethical approval.

The result is an undeclared new social pact: *we give you our wealth, you give us your trust.*

But it is a pact that redistributes no power—it merely relocates it. Capital presents itself as the solution to the very problems it helps generate; and politics, impoverished and dependent, accepts this offer of collaboration with gratitude, without realizing that collaboration is a form of control.

Yet the final paradox is that such a system cannot endure. No society can sustain itself for long on a language that promises what it does not deliver. The rhetoric of fiscal justice works only as long as it remains ambiguous; but every economic crisis, every social fracture, every geopolitical shock forces it to reveal what it truly is: not a project of equity, but a stabilizing mechanism.

And so the question before us is no longer "Who should pay?", but something far more uncomfortable: *How long can a morality that reassures everyone while changing nothing continue to function?*

The answer is unwritten, but one thing is certain: the next major political transformation of the West will arise precisely from this blind spot—from the moment when the redistributive fiction is no longer sufficient to contain collective anxiety and the fragility of States.

The task of politics, if it wishes to recover meaning, will no longer be to tax the rich, but to return to society what it has lost: the capacity to imagine an order not defined by wealth, but by responsibility. Not a moralistic order, but a real one.

For social justice is not a proclamation; it is a balance that must be built. And it cannot be built as long as power retains the privilege of defining the language through which justice is spoken.

By the same author at Ad Veritatem

Ukraine, Russia, and NATO: Exposing the Myths Behind Pro-Russian and Anti-Western Narratives

Beyond the China Myth: Inside — and Against — Keyu Jin's The New China Playbook

About the Author

Marco Deuropa was shaped by the moral and political philosophy of the twentieth century—a century he considers the great school of responsibility. From Hannah Arendt he learned that politics begins with the courage to face reality without illusion; from Simone Weil, that justice can never be reduced to rhetoric; from Emmanuel Levinas, that ethics is an obligation toward the other, not an ornament of power.

Equally formative were the voices of those who confronted evil without letting it remake them: Aleksandr Solzhenitsyn and Václav Havel, witnesses to a Europe in which truth was not a discourse but a wound. Dietrich Bonhoeffer, who paid with his life for fidelity to conscience; and thinkers such as Romano Guardini and Luigi Pareyson, who taught him to see culture not as self-indulgence but as a form of responsibility.

With these roots, Marco Deuropa examines the moral climate of our time—a morality that often ceases to be truth and becomes strategy. His books explore the transformation of contemporary power, where ethics bends to convenience and justice becomes a language rather than a principle.

www.ingramcontent.com/pod-product-compliance
Lightning Source LLC
LaVergne TN
LVHW100321210926
848480LV00003B/1203